IN THE BEGINNING GOD

IN

THE

BEGINNING

GOD

by William M. Logan

JOHN KNOX PRESS
Richmond, Virginia

Library of Congress Catalog Card Number: 57-11746

TO MY WIFE

FOREWORD

The change in contemporary thought regarding the early chapters of Genesis is one of the most striking that has occurred in the renewal of Biblical faith. Once men were sharply divided between those who accepted these chapters as literal history and those who rejected them as primitive superstition. These two views seemed to exhaust the logical possibilities. Now there is a great and growing tendency to recognize a third alternative, an alternative as different from one of these as from the other.

This third way arises from the recognition that the inspired authors of the stories in Genesis were really dealing with the universal human predicament. The stories are not accounts of debatable events which happened too long ago to permit any valid process of verification, but are, instead, accounts of the nature of enduring human problems. These accounts are so universally accurate that they are essentially dateless. The story of the garden and its famous residents is the story of earth and its human inhabitants. Always moral insight comes at a price; always man differs from the beasts in that he asks what he ought to do; always man's freedom involves attendant dangers of great seriousness. Man can rise higher than any beast, but he can also sink lower than a beast can fall.

Genesis is the philosophy of human paradox in narrative form. The book tells of the greatness of man and of the littleness of man, and it tells of both together. It is the story of pride, of murder, of deceit, and of penitence. Man, whether male or female, protects the ego by placing blame upon another. Pride leads both to material failure and to a confusion of tongues whether the time be then or now. All of this is made credible by the contemporary procession of events in a technological age.

When William Logan began to feel the profundity of this approach to the ancient stories it gave a new depth to his preaching. He found that such a way of thinking was largely unfamiliar to the men and women sitting in the pews, even though it was well understood by advanced theologians. Accordingly, he decided to try to prepare for publication a set of meditations based upon the chapters which appear at the beginning of our printed Bibles. He found that, though many people have read the early chapters of Genesis many times, the mere reading of these has not produced understanding. Some people start again with Genesis each time they make a new decision about regular Bible reading, but they soon bog down because they lack a key to understanding. This key, as William Logan well knows, is the recognition that what we face is a highly intelligent account of the perennial human situation.

I am very glad that William Logan has undertaken to give something of great value to the average thoughtful reader. Years ago, when I was writing in the beautiful hill country where the author of the present volume was then a pastor, I came to admire his spoken word and now I am happy to be able to commend his written word.

ELTON TRUEBLOOD

PREFACE

This book is an attempt to share some reflections on the first eleven chapters of Genesis. It began with a conviction that there must be more significance to them than I had previously thought or than was commonly acknowledged. When I began studying them more seriously, I found some difficulty in securing the kind of help for which I was looking. In most instances the material would be either a purely devotional probing of one small aspect of a passage, or it would plunge at great and learned detail into the technical depths of textual criticism. Not for one moment would I disparage either approach, each most valuable and helpful in its own way; but it was not that for which I was looking. Nor was a verse-by-verse commentary the answer.

It seemed to me that a continuous narrative, unbroken by analysis of textual sources and not pausing for detailed wrestling with all obscure passages, might catch a little more readily the charm and wisdom of these glorious stories. This book is an effort to provide that narrative. Since its beginning years ago an increasing number of excellent studies of Genesis have appeared, all of which have enriched my appreciation of its relevance to today's world. It is hoped that this volume may in its own way help to call attention to this part of God's revelation.

I am especially grateful to two men: J. S. Whale, whose fellowship for a brief period in Cambridge and then whose book *Christian Doctrine* first stimulated the interest in this portion of Genesis, and D. Elton Trueblood, who as a "temporary parishioner" in my congregation for a month first urged the development of a book from the material in hand. I am further indebted to a great number of writers whom I cannot now specifically thank. The notes made over the past ten years were not originally intended for publication; and consequently, having lived so long with these thoughts, I have been unable to be sure of separating quotation from home-grown product.

A thorough student of Genesis may well be appalled at the almost complete ignoring of problems of textual criticism. A casual reader of Genesis may wish that some fascinatingly obscure passages had been dealt with more thoroughly. I believe I am at least aware of the major questions of textual criticism, and I certainly have as much curiosity about the obscure passages as any person; but one purpose has dominated this writing. It is similar to a primary rule of landscape painting: locate your main masses first, and proportions and details will fall into place more easily. I am concerned that the major truths of these stories be set out, free from distracting details. If I have correctly stated these major truths and have thereby made easier the appropriation of them into the lives of people, I shall be most grateful. If I have misunderstood, and thereby cause others to search out and expound the corrections, my purpose will still be accomplished.

WILLIAM M. LOGAN

Austin, Texas
May, 1957

CONTENTS

ONE

The Nature of the
Early Chapters of Genesis

EVEN a casual reader of the book of Genesis notices a distinct, though unannounced, change of tone at the beginning of chapter twelve. With that chapter begins the story of Abraham and his descendants. From that point on the record has a more concrete sound. It moves more slowly and gives more details. It does not cover a thousand years in a single breath. It slows down to a pace with which we can keep up as it traces the life story of men and a nation.

In contrast, the first eleven chapters of Genesis are epic in their scope. Their sweep is tremendous. Incomprehensible periods of time are covered in a few words. Stupendous events are described with the brevity and matter-of-factness of a child's fairy story. Many people have been misled by that simple, naive style into treating these stories as about as relevant to modern life as the stories of the Brothers Grimm: interesting, but not to be taken as containing any serious truth.

Nevertheless, when one begins to study these tales, he finds emerging the basic facts that underlie all his life as an individual and as a member of society. Like the overture to an opera these chapters introduce themes whose elaboration is still in process and whose development brings joy or sorrow in the life of modern man. A great part of the charm of the stories lies in their child's-tale simplicity, a simplicity that is probably the mark of master storytellers who, from generation to generation, passed along these tales long before they were ever written down. The inspiration that guided their final recording also guided the preservation through all preceding generations of the priceless gem of truth, of which the details of the story are the setting, the better to display its facets.

It is that central gem that is the object of our consideration here. The man who sent word to a pastor that he would join his church if the pastor could tell him where Cain got his wife probably deserved the answer the pastor sent back, that until he was worried about something other than that part of the story, he was not ready to join the church. Many have made this man's mistake of concerning themselves so much with the mounting, that the jewel for which the mounting was fashioned has been ignored.

Much of the time such ignoring is not willful; it comes from a misconception of the purpose and nature of the Genesis record. An archaeologist, on the eve of the publication of a valuable and helpful book he had written, recently sought advice on whether he, as a devout churchman, was doing the right thing in releasing a publication which might disturb the faith of his readers. The book contained nothing but a factual classification and dating of various artifacts gathered in intensive research over one area of the country, all done by the soundest accepted principles. Yet it seemed to him, and he feared it might also seem to his readers, that he must close his mind to the early chapters of Genesis in order to declare the obvious evidence of the archaeology which he had studied devotedly for fifty years.

Such tensions are tragic and utterly unnecessary. There simply can be no conflict between science, properly defined, and Genesis, for Genesis is not concerned with scientific questions at all. These early stories transmit a revelation about the nature of man that is independent of date and that can never grow old. Those of us who received instruction in the physical sciences even a generation ago would be in grave danger of failing any high school examination in the same subject today, for every new discovery in the physical sciences makes obsolete an old hypothesis. Thus no modern school would teach, except as a curiosity, the physics of Aristotle or the astronomy of Ptolemy.

Yet it would, and does, teach the plays of Aeschylus and Shakespeare and the Dialogues of Plato. Why? Because fundamental human existence has not changed. That which makes us *man* is just what it has always been. The hydrogen bomb is our longer spear, given to us by a science that has utterly supplanted Aristotle's physics; but its use is under the domination of passions identical with those of the characters of Aeschylus. Similarly, and even more profoundly, the basic human predicament described in the early chapters of Genesis has not been modified by any development of modern science, and it makes no difference at all whether the writer of those chapters believed in a cosmology consonant with our present scientific description.

The writer here was not seeking to write a textbook of history or of science. If anyone is in search of accurate information regarding the age of this earth, or its relation to the sun, moon, and stars, or regarding the order in which plants and animals appeared upon it, he is referred to the latest textbooks in astronomy, geology, and paleontology. No one dreams of referring a serious student of these subjects to the Bible as a source of information. The subject of creation, of the beginning of man upon earth, was not approached from that side at all; and if we are to understand what is written here, we must read these chapters not as a chronological, astronomical, geological, biological statement, but as a moral and spiritual conception.

It is absolutely essential that we understand clearly the nature of the message of the early Genesis stories in order that the light that is in them may illumine our own needs. These stories throb with a message that only our spiritual hearing can detect. They are parables, not history or explanations. Consequently, they continually imply that beyond the words is a meaning which "he that hath ears to hear" may hear. But there is no attempt to formulate intellectual propositions to state basic truths. Instead, the method is that of poetic imagery and symbolism. The aim is to awaken in man an awareness of his existence in the presence of God and of his utter dependence upon God. The stories are told in such manner that when I read them, I realize that I am not reading an account of history; I am looking in a mirror! This is not Adam I am reading about; this is myself. This is not a tower built long ago in a faraway country; this is my own society in action, and I am part and parcel of that society.

The ability to provoke this intense personal response is a mark of divine inspiration and is one of the things that sets the Biblical record apart from similar material we possess from other sources. Marked parallels are found, for example, in the Babylonian and the even older Sumerian stories of creation. A reader who notes only the similarities of detail in the order and processes of creation may conclude that the Genesis account is but another version of an ancient legend common throughout the Middle East. Closer study reveals remarkable difference. The evoking of personal response is utterly lacking in the Babylonian account. The reader remains merely a reader, though perhaps intrigued by the ingenuity of an interesting fable. In the Genesis account the whole world of thought is different. Many details are similar, but the thought is completely inverted. Instead of showing how God can be made to serve the purposes of man, Genesis portrays man as utterly dependent upon and responsible to God. Moreover, instead of numerous gods and goddesses personifying various forces of nature, there stands at the very beginning *one* God who creates matter out of nothing, not just fashioning it out of pre-existent material after the manner of a human craftsman, and who exists independently of all cosmic matter.

With such difference apparent in the meaning derived from similar sets of details, it becomes obvious that the significant thing is not the origin of those details but the use to which the writer puts them. Not only their origin but also the details themselves were of subordinate significance, for they were not recited as data on the basis of which conclusions were to be drawn but rather were media to transmit spiritual truths. In conveying these spiritual truths to the people of his day he was using an account of creation which they could all understand. If, by supernatural instruction, the writer of Genesis had been told of the countless millions of years that went into the formation of this earth, God would have short-circuited, so to speak, that great gift of His to man, the gift of acquiring scientific knowledge. Moreover, and what is more important, if this writer had mingled with his teaching regarding God an exact and detailed account of how this world had come into existence in a material way as science now teaches us, in all probability he would have been utterly discredited among his contemporaries, and what he had to say about God would have been rejected along with his premature science, which would have been fantastically unbelievable to his age.

So far as merely physical knowledge goes, there is probably little in the Genesis account that was new to the contemporaries of the writer. He simply was using familiar knowledge, and the more familiar the better, as the vehicle for conveying his faith in the unity and love and wisdom of God. He was laying a firm foundation for the history of God's relation to man. That was his purpose, and that is what he accomplished. For that reason, no changes in our knowledge of physical truth can at all affect the teaching of these chapters. What they teach regarding the relation of man to God is independent of the physical details in which the teaching is embodied, and can just as easily be attached to the most modern statement of the physical origin of the world and of man. If, for example, it should be announced tomorrow that all previous geological theories have been proved wrong, and that this earth came into being in a period of six days of twenty-four hours each, my faith would be neither strengthened nor weakened. My faith is not attached to the physical facts of geology; it is attached to the relation of the living God with man. I turn to these chapters, not to study science, but to begin learning the history and meaning of God's revelation of Himself and of His will toward men. That is the purpose for which they were written. "The Lord is my shepherd" may be found to be truth whether the earth is flat or round. The Bible writers bowed respectfully to the science of the day, which ever changes, and hurried on to utter the word of a Presence, which in all change is ever the same.

It will seem to many who have always so understood these stories that such a laboring of the point is unnecessary, for it has been repeated again and again in commentary after commentary. Nevertheless, there is good reason to believe that a majority of persons do not have this perception. It is even quite common for university professors of geology to acquire a reputation for great wit in ridiculing the Genesis account of creation, and for wide-eyed freshmen to be launched on a career of "sophisticated" iconoclasm by this daring assault of "science" upon "superstition." If the youth seeks parental guidance about the problem, too often he is assured somewhat vaguely that "there is an answer" or that "some things just have to be taken by faith." Thus there is the implication that the Biblical record is a sort of second-rate source of knowledge and that early Genesis contains pathetically primitive guesses at scientific truth.

Far from being second-rate, these stories are the work of spiritual adults while many of us are still spiritual adolescents. They represent a maturity of perception of the highest quality. With a reverence born of intimate knowledge of God they speak of Him and His characteristics with an artless familiarity that occasions some difficulty in our own thinking simply because we are not wise, being only "wise in our own conceits." The human sin of pride, whose work we shall be observing at greater length very shortly, is operating here. Enraptured by the admitted wonders of modern scientific achievement, we easily slip into thinking that there was no knowledge worthy of the name in "pre-scientific" days. In some areas of knowledge this may have a measure of truth, but continuous, evolutionary progress is by no means evident in every realm of wisdom. Indeed, the artificiality, the complexity, and the luxury of advancing civilization have obscured much of our understanding of true values and inner meanings. Witness the immense problem of mental illness. Is that growing affliction a testimony to the fact that we understand ourselves and the world in which we live better than the ancients? Again and again the Hebrew prophets called upon their people to shake off the blinding obsession of external artificialities and to go back to abiding fundamentals. They were true conservatives, in the sense that they saw the necessity of conserving realities in order that real progress might be made. The fact that early Genesis speaks from a very ancient time in no way justifies any thought that its truths are obsolete.

Not only are the truths enduring, but also the method of presenting those truths defies improvement. We have already noted the power of the stories to call forth personal response. Any attempt to "explain" them will not have the same effect. It must be stated clearly that the author of this book acknowledges that fact, and that he has no misguided aims in that direction. The stories must speak for themselves. The multiplication of pages dealing with their content has a similar connotation to that which has been remarked about by historians; namely, that a sure sign of the decline of a civilization is its excessive multiplication of laws. The more numerous the laws passed, the greater the evidence that fundamental laws are being violated. The most that can be hoped for here is that a sharing of reflections on these stories will prompt others to study and teach them with greater interest and thus give the stories themselves the opportunity for speaking which they so richly deserve.

Not long ago the newspapers carried an item to the effect that a bishop in another country had made a curiously contradictory statement. To the clergy of his diocese he declared that the Bible contains "fanciful falsehoods" regarding man. Saying that proof had been found that civilization began in Europe 20,000 years ago, he continued: "In the face of such notice we cannot teach fanciful falsehoods, however poetic, literary, or symbolic, to children in our church schools. If we wish to win the confidence of our young people, we must tell them the new-found truths of the origin of man and of human civilization, and these proofs must be combined with their religious education." The contradictory element lies in the fact that the man is pleading for a combination of "new-found truths" with religious education while scorning as "fanciful false-hoods" the superb combination already available. If the creation narratives are taught in their proper significance, they furnish complementary "religious education" of the profoundest kind to "the new-found truths of the origin of man and of human civilization." They are classic masterpieces.

TWO

In the Beginning God

WHEN Daniel Webster was asked, "Mr. Webster, what is the most important thought that ever occupied your mind?" he answered, "The most important thought that ever occupied my mind was that of my individual responsibility to God." [1] When we ask the purpose of the story of the first two chapters of Genesis, we get essentially the same answer. The writer is setting forth the relation of the world—and man in particular—to God, and God's relation to the world—and to man in particular. He is not attempting to prove the existence of God; nowhere in the Bible does any writer ever seem to have had the idea that that was necessary. It seems to be assumed, rather, that man's awareness of and response to God is the very thing that makes man *man* and distinguishes him from a mere animal. "He is a person standing all the time in personal relationship to God. It is that relationship which constitutes him—MAN. . . . Man is distinctly man at all only because—whether he knows it or not, whether he likes it or not—he stands, right down to the innermost core and essence of his being, in the profoundest possible relationship to God all the time in an order of persons." [2] "Man is man because he is able to receive a word from the dimension of the eternal." [3]

The writer of Genesis underscores his words, "In the beginning God created"; that is, "before the creation of anything God created out of nothing the whole universe." The Hebrew word used here for "created" is one that is used only of God in the Bible. It implies something utterly beyond human imitation or comprehension. In the myth of creation in Plato's *Timaeus* the divine craftsman fashions the world out of matter already present, just as a potter makes vessels out of clay. That dualistic conception of the world is as far as unaided philosophy could go. Creation "out of nothing" is a conception introduced by revelation; it is an essentially miraculous work that can be accomplished only by the living God. All things, though definitely distinct from Him, are utterly dependent on Him. This is decidedly not an answer to the question of world origins in a scientific sense, and it does not compete with anything science may say about the temporal process by which things have come to be what they are. It probably involves the idea that time itself is part of creation. There is a sense, then, in which we must try not to regard the creation story (nor any other story at which we shall be looking) as an event in history at all. Our usual conception of history is that it is a story of human evolution and advance. That is a true story from its own point of view. But "creation out of nothing" is a story of divine action, a proclamation of "the mighty works of God." It is far greater than merely the description of the beginning of a chain of events.

"The Christian doctrine of creation does not arise from our interest in explaining the world or accounting for its 'origin' at some approximately datable time in the cosmic past. The doctrine of creation 'out of nothing' is not a scientific description of the beginning of the time series. Here, no scientific statements are possible. 'Before Abraham was, I am' (John 8:58). Belief in the creation means a way, *the* way, of understanding the present world. It is an act of faith (Hebrews 11:3). ['Through faith we understand that the worlds were framed by the word of God, so that things which are seen were not made of things which do appear.'] Creation out of nothing is not to be understood as an historical event but as a description of existence. Here is truth which we receive by faith; we do not conceive it at all, since it transcends the utmost limit of all human conceiving. The doctrine of creation out of nothing is not a cosmological theory, but an expression of our adoring sense of the transcendent majesty of God and of our utter dependence upon Him." [4]

The majestic "lead line" has opened the story: "In the beginning God created the heaven and the earth." Now the details are filled in. The same tone of majesty carries on, creating a mood strikingly appropriate to the magnitude of the theme. Stage by stage creation unfolds. It unfolds in response to a word: "And God said, Let there be . . . and it was so." In this simple manner the absolute power of God is exalted. Here is no artificer laboring with a mass of pre-existent material; this is the Creator at work. He utters His will, and it is instantly accomplished.

This emphasis upon the creative word of God is certain to remind us of the deliberate parallelism in the opening words of the Gospel of John: "In the beginning was the Word, and the Word was with God, and the Word was God. The same was in the beginning with God. All things were made by him; and without him was not any thing made that was made. . . . And the Word was made flesh, and dwelt among us . . . full of grace and truth." In the climax of God's revelation of Himself to men the creative Word which was active in the first creation became incarnate so that "if any man be in Christ Jesus, there has been a new creation." [5]

Each stage of creation is prefaced by the words, "And God said"; and each stage, except the first two, is followed by the words, "and God saw that it was good." That there is no significance to these omissions is indicated by the words which sum up the whole mighty act: "And God saw every thing that he had made, and, behold, it was very good." Thus is made the affirmation that the world as created by God was in no way defective or marred by evil.

The essential fact in this entire narrative is that all things existing are the creation of God, who works in an orderly, progressive, purposeful manner. They have not just grown of themselves, nor have they arisen from a fortuitous concourse of atoms; they have been called into being out of nothing by a presiding Intelligence and an originating Will. Perhaps the only reason why this poetic account marks off stages in the act of creation is to emphasize the fact that God's workings are orderly, progressive, and purposeful.

This orderliness of God is the foundation of all our learning. So-called "natural laws" are but descriptions of the dependable consistency of God. Though sometimes they seem to be fetters upon us, forcing us into necessary accommodation to them, they are really our freedom. If it were never certain from one day to the next whether gravitation would pull sideways, down, or up, this complex world would dissolve in uninhabitable chaos. The natural sciences proceed by a method of observation, induction, experiment, and verification. What they arrive at is a description of the reliability of God. They are adding more details to the basic fact that "in the beginning God created." It is said that the naturalist Agassiz customarily began his lectures with the words, "Gentlemen, we shall now seek to think God's thoughts after Him." Such a remark betrays a spiritual perception that could be desired as the possession of every man. G. K. Chesterton once said a thing that is instructive in its contradiction. He said, "The sun does not rise because of the rotation of the earth. The sun rises because God says, 'Get up and do it again.' " The more prosaic language of the Westminster Confession of Faith states the same thing by declaring that by the sovereign decrees of God "the liberty or contingency of second causes [is not] taken away, but rather established." [6]

Though this conception of God the Creator sounds familiar enough, there is a depth of meaning in its simplicity and an uncompromising demand about its nature that is sometimes missed, even by the most devout. There are prevalent other conceptions of God, less majestic than this, elements of which have crept most surprisingly into the thinking of many Christians. We may not know the technical names of these philosophies, but many of us have uncritically accepted some of their teachings.

One of those philosophies has been called Deism. Deistic thinking conceives of God as the great First Cause of all that is, but it isolates Him from all present working in the world except through the functioning of divinely instituted laws. In this view, creation is a past act in which God wound up the universe like a clock and then retired to a lonely inaccessibility, leaving the world to run in fixed manner according to the rules and characteristics originally ordained.

The intense anthropomorphism of Genesis is itself a strong antagonist of any such philosophy. That mouth-filling word seems inevitable in any discussion of the Old Testament revelation of God. Long though it is, it is shorter than an explanation of its meaning; and knowledge of that meaning is important, for it represents a trait of Hebrew thought that is significant and helpful. Anthropomorphism is a representation of God in human guise. Its use is a testimonial to the personal nature of God, the direct opposite of the implications of Deism. But there is a message as well as a technique here. Beginning with the story of creation and continuing on every succeeding page, the Bible sets forth an account of God's relation to the world in a continuous act. "In him we live and move and have our being." [7] Apart from His eternal creativity the whole world would at once cease to be. Far from being a blind, inexorable, merciless machine, this world is the continuous expression of the concern of a God who sees everything that He makes as "very good."

Identified specifically, this alien philosophy is readily rejected by Christians. But what about the feeling that you are caught in the grip of blind, mechanical forces and that you are the helpless victim of circumstances? Have you tried the deep discipline and understanding of prayer, or do you feel that the universe runs by laws that rigidly limit the power of prayer so that the only thing we can be safe in praying is that we may be humbly submissive to those laws? That, you see, is Deism rearing its ugly head, the idea of the universe as a wound-up machine with God Himself cut off from taking heed of your plight, by laws set in operation by Himself. Prayer has its rules, but not its limits. This world is not a blind machine; it is a divine purpose. There is no place in it for blank despair, either for yourself or for the world in general.

The Genesis conception of the nature of creation is also decidedly distinct from a second philosophy, Pantheism, which views the universe as an emanation of God rather than a creation by Him, conceiving of God as creating all things out of Himself, out of His own substance. Pantheism depersonalizes God into a World Soul, abstract and unknowable; the whole of things is God. But to say, "God created," immediately asserts that, though the world is an expression of God's character and will, it is distinct from Him and fashioned for purposes determined and guided by a Person. God is sovereign over and distinct from everything else that is.

Some who like to classify themselves as Christians take an esthetic approach to their religion that is perilously close to that slippery, hard-to-define philosophy of Pantheism. Such are the nature-worshipers, who commune with God better on the beach or in the woods or on the emerald expanse of the golf green than in church. Or if they are in church, the music must be faultless, the temperature perfect, and the minister poised, polished, and interesting, but not excited. After all, God is perfection, God is all things in harmonious balance. Others like a "positive" religion, one that is "broad," without any prohibitions. Since all things are God, then it must be all right to experience all things. All such Pantheists need to be reminded that in morals as well as in algebra there is a minus as well as a plus sign. Some experiences subtract from what we had before, rather than add to it. This world is dependent upon God, but distinct from Him. God resides not so much *in* this world as *above* it. The instinct that causes us to think of heaven as "above" is not literally true, but it is spiritually true. God is sovereign over this world and infinitely beyond the sum of all of it.

Still another philosophy, Dualism, conceives of God as the Great Artificer, laying His hands to the fashioning of a universe out of some sort of pre-existent material which is independent of Him and in some sense hostile to Him. Evil thus becomes a bit of unfinished work on the part of God, a sort of loose end not yet tucked in or a particularly stubborn bit of material that has

broken out of bounds. The universe is a sort of cosmic battle-
ground, the strife raging between spirit and matter, between God
and chaos. In the fourth and fifth centuries of our era a very
persistent form of this philosophy was formulated by a man
called Manichaeus who had a wide following in western Asia and
eastern Europe. Manichaeism taught that the world began from
an accidental mixing of two absolutely contrasting elements, one
radically good and one radically bad, but both eternal. Man was
the center of the conflict between the two, and those who observed the strictest rules of this religious sect were forbidden to
plant a tree, to build a house, to engage in any kind of manufac-
turing industry, to marry, or to engage in any kind of occupation
which might interfere with the progress of the realm of light,
which was felt to be far above any such sensual indulgences.

Manichaean dualism is a lively current philosophy. Its prevalent form is the attitude of restricting religion solely to the
sanctuary in "spiritual" matters, while denying its relevance to
business, politics, social problems, and other "practical" matters
of life. This is utterly foreign to the spirit with which the Bible
begins and which pervades it to the end. The anthropomorphism
of Hebrew thought is no more than a determination to keep all
thought of God and all talk about God on a personal, practical
level. It refuses to speak of God—or for that matter, of man—
in universals or generalities of abstract concepts. Its certainties
are certainties of relationship and action. God created; God is
the One who brought Israel out of Egypt; God keeps His covenant "to a thousand generations." Similarly, man, when he is
obedient to God, is in right relationships with his earthly environment and with his fellows. "And God saw every thing
that he had made, and, behold, it was very good." Life cannot be
partitioned into "sacred" and "secular." This world is a unity in
God, and He is sovereign over it all. He is Lord of a man's
business, his pleasure, his politics, or He is not that man's Master,
for only a tiny fraction of even a most devout man's life is spent
directly in so-called "spiritual" matters.

Thus in many subtle ways pagan philosophies mislead from the

simple profundity of "In the beginning God created." This is
God's world, and God, though immanent in it and continually
sustaining it, created it by His own deliberate, purposeful, mysterious will and absolute power. Moreover, the whole procession
of the narrative is a description of a world prepared for man.
He is the crown of creation. Toward his advent the entire story
is pointed. The climax is reached in the words: "And God said,
Let us make man in our image, after our likeness: and let them
have dominion . . . So God created man in his own image, in
the image of God created he him; male and female created he
them. . . . And the Lord God formed man of the dust of the
ground, and breathed into his nostrils the breath of life; and man
became a living soul." [8]

Some word of comment on the use of the plural pronoun
"us" is well-nigh demanded here. The word used in this passage
is the ordinary Hebrew word for God, *Elohim*. It is plural in
form, but that fact is not at all to be taken as a survival element
from an ancient polytheistic religion nor as a foreshadowing of
the doctrine of the Trinity in any direct way. The conception
of the Trinity did, however, mature out of the deep insight expressed in this plural form. The Genesis writer is expressing his
consciousness of God as a person, and a person could not exist
alone. God is not, and never was, a lonely God. He is supreme
and unique, but He is not "the Alone," as sometimes described in
Greek philosophy. We cannot, of course, imagine what God is
like; but the richness of His being is suggested by this plural
form, as though a word signifying one single being could never
be adequate to express His fullness.

Man, the high priest of the order of creation, is created by
God with an essential difference between himself and the highest
animal. One emphasis upon this is the use three times in chapter
1, verse 27, of the seldom-used Hebrew word for "create" that
is used previously only in the opening verse. Moreover, man is
created by God "in our image," and that is said of no other
portion of the created world.

It is in connection with the creation of man that we are able to see the significance of the fact that there are two creation narratives here. The second one begins at the fourth verse of chapter 2. Scholars identify readily two collateral sources of material through all the stories which we shall be studying, but any reader can see a marked difference in style and emphasis between the accounts in these first two chapters. We have already said that in the final analysis these stories must stand alone and speak their own message. In this we are adopting the apparent conviction of our ancient recorder, who made no effort to consolidate into a single account the insights which are most helpful when allowed to stand side by side.

It is only when we look at both accounts that we see the true status and condition of man. Chapter 1 sweeps its vision over all the cosmos and in that setting emphasizes the uniqueness and dignity of man, created "in the image of God." This lordly creature, Man, has "dominion" over the remainder of the created world, exercising some of God's powers as His representative. Chapter 2 localizes its concern to Eden, and there in the garden stands man in a relation of dependence and obedience to God. He is of the same substance as the animal and vegetable world, formed "of the dust of the ground," his existence depending on the "breath of life" which he has only as the gift of God. Even the name by which man is called is derived from his humble origin. The Hebrew word for man is *adam;* the word for ground is *adamah*. As for plants and animals, his dominion over them is not mentioned here; he only gives them their names.

The truth of each of these accounts is more emphatic because it stands clear in its own context, but each demands the other for completeness in describing the nature of man. They are complementary and not in any sense contradictory. So noble and yet so earthy, man cannot be understood by assuming that he is either one or the other. The optimistic humanism, now largely shattered, that assumed that man would inevitably rise higher and higher and exhibit more and more his essential deity, was looking only at the lordly nature of man. A materialistic philosophy such as Communism looks only at the "dust" side of man's nature, assuming that he is nothing more than an animal. Anyone who would understand man must see him in the totality of his nature as described by these two accounts of his creation, standing side by side.

Thus this vivid, poetic account presents the essential nature of this complex creature, Man. The immensity of the universe about him dwarfs him into insignificance, yet, unabashed, he analyzes the stars with his spectroscope, weighs them with his mathematical computations, brings them near with his bigger and bigger telescopes, and lays methodical plans to transport his person nearer to them by rocket ships. At the other end of the scale even the atom in its minuteness is not inviolate from his prying; and when he has discovered all the elements present in nature, he proceeds to create new ones by bombarding the old with high-speed neutrons. Man is superior to the remainder of the universe because there is a qualitative difference between him and it. Vast and glorious as it is, the sun cannot think God's thoughts after Him. It can fulfill God's purpose, but it cannot exercise conscious choice to do so. Man alone can answer God's address, hear His law, and make or withhold his conscious and deliberate response. Therefore, man alone is conscious of his responsibility before God and is aware that he stands in the presence and under the judgment of God.

To the writer of the Genesis story the likeness of God in man is most manifest in man's sharing in the Creator's dominion over the remainder of creation. "And God said, Let us make man in our image, after our likeness: and let them have dominion . . . So God created man in his own image . . . And God blessed them, and God said unto them, Be fruitful, and multiply, and replenish the earth, and subdue it: and have dominion . . . over every living thing that moveth upon the earth." [9] Those words describe what man *is*, a creature made "in the image of God," and what is his *function*, to "have dominion." But just here lurks man's deadly peril; his high privilege tempts him to forget that his dominion is a *delegated* dominion. He is lord of creation and ruler of nature not in his own right or to work his own will; he is charged with

working God's will and is responsible to God for his steward-
ship. Mark well this ordained relationship, for beginning in
chapter 3 of Genesis and continuing to today's newspaper you
may review the sad spectacle of man's age-long effort to subdue
the earth to his own ends and not to God's glory.

It is worth noting, even if only in passing, that this divine
commission to dominion does not extend to dominion over other
men. That omission seems to say, "One is your master, even
God." Whenever man seeks to extend his influence over other
men solely for the purpose of dominion, blight rather than blessing is the result. Man's relation to man is horizontal rather than
vertical. "My service to him shall not flow like a stream, as if
from a higher to a lower level, but shall move as the tide moves
across the bosom of the ocean; that is, on a level, drawn by the
attraction of a Power above." [10]

To illustrate some of the far-reaching implications of insisting
on the primacy of God, as this account of creation does, we
might look at a debate in print which appeared some years ago
between Robert Hutchins, then Chancellor of the University of
Chicago, and James B. Conant, then President of Harvard.[11] This
discussion dealt with the structure of a university curriculum.
It was based on the recognition that men in leadership must determine what ideals they wish to propose for their country.
Human values must be ordered so that some things are judged to
be better than others. But whence does this standard of values
come? Are some values objectively higher than others and are
they always higher?

Hutchins insisted that there are some values that *are* objectively higher than others. If not, then values are capricious and
changeable. The standard for saying, "X is valuable," becomes
simply, "I desire X." Under such a conception, philosophy and
theology become worse than useless in a university. But if God
is and this is a God-sustained world, continued Hutchins, some
truths must be of more importance than others and some subjects
more important than others. For example, the quest for moral
and spiritual truths is more important than, though not a sub-

stitute for, the quest for truths about soil conservation or business management.   Thus to subordinate some values to higher values is not to deny them any value at all, but rather to recognize their *real* value.   He would, then, put theology at the center of a university curriculum as the unifying discipline for all else.

Conant, on the other hand, maintained in this debate that there are no general truths that determine a university curriculum. Instead, a curriculum should be shaped by public pressure and desires.   One subject is as good as another if public pressure says so.   Thus, as industrialization increases, the public demand is that agriculture and shop technique and petroleum engineering be put "on a par" with theology, philosophy, and law.

But, retorted Hutchins, "there is no difference whatsoever in denying all religious and theological truth and in saying that agriculture is on a par with the divinity school.   If God does not exist, then theology is of less value than agriculture.   In fact, it is worthless.   If God exists, then theology is more important in a university curriculum than agriculture."

The point in citing these words is not that we are setting ourselves to decide which of these thoughtful, able men is right.   The point is that "In the beginning God created . . . " is far more than a mere statement of origins.   It embraces a whole way of thinking of life.   The sovereign God of Genesis must be reckoned with wherever one turns in life.

It is precisely this confrontation of man by God in every aspect of his existence that is the burden of the revelation in these chapters of Genesis.   They communicate the awareness of our existence in relation to God.   God is addressing us in these pages, not to disclose any scientific knowledge about the origin of the world nor to promulgate any philosophical ideas, but to make known to us the utter dependence of ourselves and our world upon Him.   Furthermore, He addresses us as a Person, whom to trust is to know.

With a woodenheaded literalness we have taken the inspired, majestic poetical images of these chapters and tried to turn them into pages of a plodding textbook of physical science.   One might as well take the words of Psalm 91, "He shall cover thee with his feathers, and under his wings shalt thou trust," and try to turn them into the pattern of an exact physical portrait of God. Or one might as well maintain that to enter into the praise of Psalm 114 one must believe that "the mountains skipped like rams, and the little hills like lambs" at a point twenty miles northeast of Jerusalem on April 10, 2000 B.C. Poetic images do not become "dated" or outmoded like scientific hypotheses. Man's relation to God and to his fellow man is a permanent relation, and to voice such a relation Genesis uses the imagery of a literary form which can become alive to the imagination of every generation and speak with the ever-sounding voice of the Living God.

Recently Dr. Jesse L. Greenstein, an astrophysicist, and Dr. William A. Fowler, a physicist, announced the hypothesis that the universe came into being by slow evolution from hydrogen atoms over five and one-half billion years ago. This is in contrast with another theory of a "cosmic explosion" origin of the universe a mere four and one-half billion years ago. But these eminent scientists said also very frankly, "With our theory the mystery of creation is as great as ever."

As man's probing of the universe reveals multiplying mystery, one reads with greater adoration, "In the beginning God created the heaven and the earth." And the conclusion grows stronger that any discussion of the works of the Living God should properly end in worship: "Like as a father pitieth his children, so the Lord pitieth them that fear him. For he knoweth our frame; he remembereth that we are dust. As for man, his days are as grass: as a flower of the field, so he flourisheth. For the wind passeth over it, and it is gone; and the place thereof shall know it no more. But the mercy of the Lord is from everlasting to everlasting upon them that fear him, and his righteousness unto children's children; to such as keep his covenant, and to those that remember his commandments to do them. . . . Bless the Lord, all his works in all places of his dominion: bless the Lord, O my soul." (Psalm 103.)

THREE

The Garden of Eden

GENESIS 3

THE first chapter of Genesis closes its account of creation with the words, "And God saw every thing that he had made, and, behold, it was very good." The same perfection is implied in the second chapter in the words, "And out of the ground made the Lord God to grow every tree that is pleasant to the sight, and good for food." The perfection of all creation is epitomized in "a garden eastward [that is, in the direction of Babylonia, the oldest civilization known to the Hebrews] in Eden." There God puts "the man whom he had formed" in a setting "where every prospect pleases," [1] where food is no problem, and where useful, pleasant occupation fills each day as man sets about doing his appointed task "to dress it and to keep it."

Such is the setting for the beginning of chapter 3, a setting far different from that in which the sons of Adam live today. "Change and decay in all around I see." [2] When we say that someone needs to face "the facts of life," we usually put it "the *hard* facts of life." We may not go so far as to say, as has one cynical observer, that life is "nasty, poor, brutish, and short"; but we readily admit that it is no idyll. Beautiful dreams and ideals have a hard time surviving. Dick Sheppard, a chaplain in the First World War, has told of a bitter bit of irony out of his own experience. During the war a young soldier was shot through the neck and died in Sheppard's arms. The last words the young fellow spoke were about the child his wife was soon to bear him. "If it's a boy," he whispered, "I'm glad he won't have to go through this. This is a war to end war, isn't it?" And Dick Sheppard comforted him, saying, "Yes, a war to end war."

He, too, believed that it was. Yet at the time he told this story on a visit to America, the child that had been born was twenty years old, dressed in a soldier's uniform, drilling somewhere in England preparatory to entering battle in a still more terrible holocaust. Such is the fate of so many of our noblest dreams and highest aspirations. Something surely has happened to Eden, and Genesis describes the nature of what has happened. The story is in chapter 3.

This is a story so marvelous that a child can read it with fascination, while a learned scholar who has ranged far and wide in the world's store of science and history and philosophy can come back to it and feel that he has here the essential truth regarding the tragic career of man upon earth. This is not, however, the answer to the philosophical question of where evil comes from. The Hebrew mind was not philosophically inclined. It gloried in contemplating and declaring the acts of God, not in trying to fathom the Divine Intellect. This is a vivid portrayal of things as they are, not a theory as to how they got that way. Here is no mere scientific analysis of human nature, a de-personalized study of "Man." Here is personal knowledge about *myself*, about my dependence upon God, my estrangement from Him, my need of reconciliation to Him.

If a person approaches this story superficially, he may be led to dismiss it with amusement or contempt. A student explores the fascinating realm of biology, and he finds that biology knows nothing of two ancestors, Adam and Eve. He explores the realm of anthropology, and he finds that anthropology knows nothing of a primitive golden age as a prehistoric fact. Therefore, he may conclude that this story is nothing but a fanciful, meaningless legend.

The fact of the matter is that in all the archives of mankind this may well be the most important document. One deeply perceptive student of human nature has voiced the opinion that if we did not have this story, we should have to invent it. The really important question about the story of the Garden of Eden is not whether it is literally, factually true in the same order of truth with which history, geography, astronomy, or geology deal, but whether it faithfully represents the truth about man's situation in history. This story is dealing with ultimate truth, which cannot be comprehended completely with the senses and therefore can be expressed only by image and symbolism and be grasped only by the imagination. Did anyone ever ask whether the Good Samaritan literally "happened"? Yet who questions its truth?

So to the story itself. What does it tell us? In this, as in all Scripture, there is no possibility of setting forth the complete "meaning." The story must make its own impact and, in its own words, must speak to us personally the truth which it has to communicate. Nevertheless, there seem to be four essential facts set forth. First, man's created position is one of happiness in intimate fellowship with God. Second, man by deliberate and willful choice disobeys God. Third, the result is estrangement from God. Fourth, the healing of the resultant breach is not impossible if God acts.

Intimate fellowship with God is set forth in a delightful and bold figure of speech. God is pictured "walking in the garden in the cool of the day," come down to take a stroll, as it were, with Adam and Eve. The very name of the garden is meant to suggest joy. Eden means "delight," "enchantment," "pleasure." The equivalent Christian symbol is "paradise." This relationship in the "garden of delight" is the Hebrew picturization of the *summum bonum*. Jesus put it in the words of His priestly prayer, "this is life eternal, that they might know thee the only true God." (John 17:3.) The great underlying fact of this close relationship is that man is capable of this kind of fellowship by act of creation of God, who into a creature formed of "dust of the ground" breathed the breath of life, "and man became a living soul."

The Hebrew word translated "soul" cannot be rendered into English in its full connotation. It is not simply a sort of life-principle, for the animals have that. The mystery of what life is is still being sought by scientists, and they have partially succeeded in creating "life" in test tubes. If these continuing experiments should result in developing animate out of inanimate matter, that still would not be the "soul" as here designated. S. R. Driver has come to the conclusion that the "soul" or "image of God" can be nothing but the gift of self-conscious reason, which is possessed by man and by no other animal. From this distinctive human gift has come progress in the arts and sciences, the power of conceiving and following intellectual and moral ideals, the faculty of distinguishing right and wrong, and the whole realm of man's unique greatness. But there is one aspect of this self-conscious reason which is most strongly implied here and which is a clue to understanding the nature of the relationship between God and man. That is the capacity of man for entering into a covenant relationship. This is in him a reflection of the nature of God, for it is the character of God to enter into a covenant with man. Made in the image of God, man has the capacity of response, of entering into a covenant. Here in Eden man has a special status and a special responsibility. His special status is that he has dominion over the earth. His responsibility is that he holds this dominion under God in a covenant relationship in which, in so far and for as long as man retains his true status as a responsible steward of God, God will grant to him full enjoyment of a fruitful and tranquil garden-world. The picture of God's coming for a customary stroll with man through the garden is a vivid symbol of covenant-partners sharing a proper order that brings joy to the hearts of both.

Against this background of ideal fellowship is projected the scene of man's deliberate and willful disobedience. "Now the serpent was more subtil than any beast of the field which the Lord God had made." The story makes no identification whatever of the serpent with Satan or a personal Devil. That conception of the origin of evil was a later development, not at all in conflict with this present account, but representing a philosophic approach not present here. This is a picture of wily, insidious temptation at work, and the symbol of it is a serpent, proverbial in Semitic lore as the representation of cunning craftiness. Perhaps a significant feature of the account is that the serpent is a part of the "beasts of the field" over which man was ordained to "have dominion." Out of the realm where man was made to be master came that which made him a bondslave.

The temptation proceeds with serpentine craftiness. First, there is the planting of uncertainty: "Did God *really* say that you should not eat of every tree? Surely you must have misunderstood." The woman bravely replies, quoting the words of the divine command. The serpent does not argue the point; uncertainty works best by being insinuated and then left to spread its own infection. Instead, his next step is the introduction of a positive denial of any bad consequences of disobedience and of active doubt of the goodness of God. The serpent said to the woman, "You shall not surely die. Rather, God knows that when you eat, your eyes will be opened, and you will be like God, knowing good and evil." Unstable because of uncertainty, poisoned by false reassurances, the woman makes her choice—obedience or disobedience of God. The picture in verse 6 is one of calculated, willful decision: "And when the woman saw that the tree was good for food, and that it was pleasant to the eyes, and a tree to be desired to make one wise, she took of the fruit thereof, and did eat, and gave also unto her husband with her; and he did eat."

"The tree of the knowledge of good and evil" is a symbol which occurs nowhere else in the Bible. Interpretation of its meaning requires careful attention to the Hebrew concepts that are employed. "Knowledge" must be understood in the Biblical rather than in the Greek sense, which is our more ordinary way of thinking of the term. It has the meaning of "practical experience" rather than "academic" or "theoretical" knowledge. Moreover, in Hebrew usage the expression "good and evil" does not necessarily imply moral good and evil; it means "everything, good and bad." "The tree of the knowledge of good and evil" has the sense, then, of "human experience in its entirety." Similarly, the serpent's tantalizing prospect that they shall be "knowing good and evil" is the prospect that they shall have the practical experience that comes by doing everything and determining for themselves what is good and what is evil, rejecting any standard set by God. This is the familiar modern allegation that ideas of right and wrong are not God-given at all, but are simply the result of human experience. Morals are not heaven-sent; they are simply patterns or habits of conduct built up out of the wisdom of the past. If "everybody does it," then it is right.

Against any such idea stands the warning, "In the day that thou eatest thereof thou shalt surely die." More will be said shortly about the relation of this to man's mortality, but this unmistakable statement from God is the background against which the woman makes her decision. There is certainly no suggestion here that the woman is more guilty than the man in yielding to temptation or that the man would have fared any better in the situation. There may be suggested, however, a most skillful acknowledgment of the superior sensitivity of women to grasp subtle intimations and to sense hidden possibilities. This is part of the distinctive excellence of woman, an excellence that is different from that of man; but in the later conversation with God, even though man tries to pass off his guilt, every character in this transaction shares an equal guilt.

In spite of the warning of the consequences the woman makes her choice. The tree is "good for food, and . . . a delight to the eyes." [3] It satisfies two legitimate desires, for food and for beauty, and in addition it can "make one wise." Those are the reasons Eve gives to herself for her actions. But the real reason is deeper, and the lesser reasons are advanced to conceal it. Her real desire is for power. She wants to be the center of the universe. She wants to be the maker of the rules. Plenty of other trees were in the garden to satisfy the need for food and beauty. This one alone, because it has attached to it a direct expression of the will of God, lures with the possibility of asserting her own will against His. With deliberate consideration, she chooses to disobey His expressed will and for it substitutes her own.

We are thus led directly into the basic nature of sin. The basic nature of sin, from which all lesser transgressions follow, is the attempt to usurp God's sole right of sovereignty. In other words, it is man's attempt to become God Himself. "Sin is not merely legal, a transgression of laws. It cannot be compared, for example, to the situation of a citizen who only breaks certain laws of the state. A man who violates the laws of a state does not thereby forfeit his citizenship. He remains a citizen, however many the laws he breaks, *so long as he recognizes the state and its right to make laws*, whether he obeys them or not. But when he proceeds to challenge the right to power of the state, he is challenging the very foundations on which both state and law rest, and there is a qualitative difference between that action and his violations of the law. It is the difference between crime and treason. Original sin is treason, not crime. In the affirmation of his own will over against God, man challenged the foundations of existence and being. He tried to appropriate the power of the state itself, so to speak. He did not merely break a law. He tried to destroy the source and foundation of all law. He compromised the basis of the moral order." [4]

It is possible that we minimize the deadly nature of sin by dwelling too long upon the meaning "a missing of the mark," which is a correct translation of one of the Greek words used in the New Testament. Sin is that, but it is also much more. The sinner is not merely an inaccurate marksman. Instead of aiming at the target, he deliberately chooses another target of his own. His deed is more than something like the error of a child in getting a wrong answer in arithmetic because his knowledge is insufficient; it is an act of *disobedience*, a deliberate choice of a self-determined way. "Sin is any want of conformity unto, or transgression of, the law of God." [5] The Genesis story of the Fall is a clear enunciation of the fact that this sin is a positive affirmation of will in disobedience of another Will. We have "lack of conformity unto the law of God" because we choose to do what we ought not to do.

The exercise of this option of self-will brought a result, but not the one Adam and Eve expected. "And the eyes of them both were opened, and they knew that they were naked; and they sewed fig leaves together, and made themselves aprons." Far from being "like God, knowing good and evil," the first fact they saw with their new-found wisdom was that "they were naked." Yet that simple fact was not, in itself, new; the new element was that they were ashamed, whereas formerly they "were not ashamed." [6] The former harmony of their relationship had become disordered. The result of their sin was estrangement from God, but the first manifestation of that estrangement was an alienation from one another. All human relationships had become disordered because their focal point was changed.

There are those who would make a great deal over the seeming close connection here between original sin and sex. It is doubtful that this is justified. The relationship between the sexes is portrayed here as poisoned by sin simply because it was the most immediate relationship existing in the scene. Very shortly other relationships will enter the picture, but all of them will be marred by the same stain of sin. This is no intimation that sex is an evil thing; it was part of God's created order and design that was seen to be "very good." "Male and female created he them," and the command to them was, "Be fruitful, and multiply, and replenish the earth." The attractions and drives associated with procreation are, therefore, not of evil but of divine origin. Moreover, Jesus Himself put a further stamp of approval upon marriage and the relationships attendant upon it: "From the beginning of the creation God made them male and female. For this cause shall a man leave his father and mother, and cleave to his wife; and they twain shall be one flesh: so then they are no more twain, but one flesh. What therefore God hath joined together, let not man put asunder." (Mark 10:6-9.)

The key to the right attitude toward sex is emphasized rather than confused by the two accounts of the creation of man and woman in chapters 1 and 2. Chapter 1 speaks of a simultaneous creation of male and female. Chapter 2 speaks of the creation of woman from a part of Adam's body, a rib. Both accounts imply that man and woman are complementary to one another and are equally important in God's design. In the account describing woman as made from the rib of man the translation, "I will make him an help meet for him," unfortunately sounds as though woman were a sort of apprentice to man. A more literal translation would be, "I will make him a help answering to him." That is, woman is one who answers, one to whom man is related in mutual responsibility. That sense of responsibility toward one another is the significant thing. When Adam and Eve belonged utterly and unselfishly to each other, "they were both naked . . . and were not ashamed." The shame arose because each, in the new-found experience of self-will, became aware that sex could become a tool of selfish gratification, ministering to self-will, and that therefore there should be a pretense of virtue, attempting to use outward means to hide inward selfishness.

The estrangement from God was exhibited when the guilty pair hid "from the presence of the Lord God amongst the trees of the garden." Not only were they ashamed in the presence of one another, but they were even more ashamed in the presence of God. The mere fig-leaf pretenses that were sufficient disguises with one another were inadequate when they confronted the Eternal Righteousness. "Try to know better than God, to break the laws of life, to imagine that our cleverness and our clutching after power can say the final word, and we stand at the end of the day dumb before the quietness of God." [7]

The healing of the breach thus created is not impossible if God acts. God is in complete and enduring control of the situation. This is exhibited first of all by consequences that come. God is the one who metes them out. The serpent is punished, and in connection therewith there is held forth the hope of man's eventual triumph over evil and temptation: "I will put enmity between thee and the woman, and between thy seed and her seed; it shall bruise thy head, and thou shalt bruise his heel."

Phillips Brooks used this passage as the text for a sermon strikingly entitled "The Giant with the Wounded Heel." Speaking about the error impatient men make in uttering crude and sweeping and unqualified epitomes of life, some saying, "It is all bad," and others saying, "It is all good," he paraphrased this verse as God's answer: "Neither! but a wounded, bruised, strong creature, not running and leaping and shouting, often crawling and creeping in its pain, but yet brave, with an inextinguishable certainty of ultimate success, fighting a battle which is full of pain but is not desperate, sure ultimately to set his heel upon his adversary's head." [8] Even though the Genesis writer had no clear vision of the coming of the Christ, he did have from God a confidence which Christian faith is correct as seeing fulfilled in the work of the Son of Man, One sent by God through the human race to slay completely and forever the power of evil.

The curse upon the serpent is far more than a mythological explanation of why snakes have no legs or why, as was supposed erroneously by early men, they eat dust. It is, rather, a perception that the mystery of the brutality of "nature, red in tooth and claw" is somehow connected with the mystery of the entry of sin into the world. The disorder produced by sin is evident in every area of the functioning of nature. Man's individual burdens are increased by it and his relationships to his world and his brethren in it are warped by its influence. For the woman, the joyous privilege of reproduction became fraught with anguish: "I will greatly multiply your pain in childbearing." [9] The widespread success of some physicians in easing the travail of childbirth by a preparatory regimen in which the prospective mother is trained in relaxation and freed from anxiety is a commentary upon the way in which distrustful fear and lack of confident faith aggravate the normal difficulties of the birth process. Man himself, whom God put into Eden "to dress it and to keep it," lost the spirit of glad co-operation with God in the labor of his days, and that labor became "sorrow," uncongenial toil, all the days of his life. Moreover, in the realm of working with others in industry and commerce, instead of a happy and deep satisfaction of fellowship in a common labor "as unto the Lord," man's lust for domination and gain for self splits his society into "dog-eat-dog" competitive groups.

"Dust thou art, and unto dust shalt thou return" is the ominous summation of the situation into which man has passed. This at once recalls the fact that "the Lord God formed man of the dust of the ground, and breathed into his nostrils the breath of life; and man became a living soul." Man is utterly and completely a creature; let him be separated from the activity of the Divine Creator, and he passes into a state of non-being. The words of verse 22 are a further addition to this emphasis, although there is an abrupt incompleteness about them: "And the Lord God said, Behold, the man is become as one of us, to know good and evil: and now, lest he put forth his hand, and take also of the tree of life, and eat, and live for ever . . ."

These two passages are consistent with the remainder of the Bible, which everywhere takes death seriously. A loose sentimentality that presumes itself to be Christian often speaks, sometimes from pulpits, of "the immortality of the soul." Immortality is a pagan philosophical concept. The great theme of Biblical revelation is resurrection, not immortality. "For the wages of sin is death; but the gift of God is eternal life through Jesus Christ our Lord." (Romans 6:23.) Paul speaks of the fact that when a man is united with Christ by faith, a "new creation" has taken place.[10] There is not in man any inherent immortality. Immortality is an attribute of God alone. Man is dust; and, for all his fantastic self-deception, he cannot make himself the equal of God. He cannot attain immortality apart from God or be lifted from his mortality by stretching out his hand to any external "tree of life." Nothing but the miracle of a new creation by the Creator Himself can confer eternal life upon man. Man is "become as one of us, to know good and evil"; that is, he has become a responsible being. But "to know good and evil" is not eternal life. "This is life eternal, that they might know thee the only true God, and Jesus Christ, whom thou hast sent." (John 17:3.)

If there is sober realism here, there is even more a joyous realism in the picture of the grace of God. Man has lost paradise, but even in his fallen state he is not abandoned by God. "Unto Adam also and to his wife did the Lord God make coats of skins, and clothed them." This is not just a whimsical bit of fancy to describe the origin of clothing. Here is man, his old innocence gone and with it his intimate fellowship with God, ashamed of his nakedness. But God's mercy provides the means by which he can still stand in the holy presence, his shame covered. This is a further picture of the unfailing initiative of God to bridge the chasm between Himself and willfully sinful man. Moreover, man is driven out from the Garden lest he eat of the fruit of "the tree of life" and "live for ever"; that is, lest he make permanent and irremediable the tragic frustration which he has brought upon himself. If this sounds like an inconsistency in view of what has been said in the preceding paragraph, bear in mind that the writer of this story is not arguing whether or not "the tree of life" has any intrinsic efficacy and whether or not man can achieve eternal life apart from God. With poetic license he is attributing to it that power for the purpose of emphasizing the grace of God, who restrains man's hand lest he "live for ever" in an unending and hopeless hell of separation from God. But would it not have been better for God to destroy the tree? No, for the symbolism carries on with the implication that the tree of life still flourishes, still available and endowed by God's power with the "healing of the nations." In the last chapter of the Bible, Revelation 22, the "tree of life" is a green and fruitful feature of the landscape of the new creation, the New Jerusalem. Defiance of God bars the way to the "tree of life"; but it does not destroy the tree itself. Guarded by "cherubim, and a flaming sword," [11] the way to it is protected for those who approach in God's own appointed path.

So ends this story which, with astonishing insight, has presented us with a prologue to the whole Biblical drama of salvation. It is a story which avoids both naive optimism and cynical pessimism in its portrayal of the nature of man. To the humanistic optimism which would regard so-called sin as nothing but an evolutionary survival from man's animal ancestry, the story in Genesis portrays sin as a deep-seated rebellion of will that is perfectly capable of keeping up with and thoroughly perverting all man's undoubtedly great advances. In answer to a cynical pessimism, it depicts the ultimate, overshadowing love and mercy of God who will not abandon man to irremediable frustration.

This story explains a great deal, but it does not explain all, especially the sinful will of man. "Man's sinful will cannot be explained: it must remain as the one completely irrational fact in a world which God created, and saw to be 'very good.' " [12] The story does not attempt to answer the question of *why* man succumbed to temptation; it simply portrays the fact that he *did* succumb. Yearning for a perfection unmarred by this sinful will, men have waxed extravagant in their imaginings of the glories of man's primitive state. Such is the nature of a famous sentence from a sermon on "Man Created in God's Image" by the eminent British clergyman Robert South about the beginning of the eighteenth century: "An Aristotle was but the rubbish of an Adam, and Athens but the rudiments of Paradise." The trouble is that absolutely no evidence from history substantiates that idea. Despite some admitted excellencies of the past which have never been surpassed, the trend of history is obviously in the other direction. We must read this story in such way as to do no violence to our God-given knowledge of history, paleontology, or biology but still to gain the benefit of its insight. The first impulse is to read it as history, for that, of course, is what it sounds like. Moreover, and more important, when an event is history, it is part of the common heritage of all men. Since sin is a universal fact of human experience, the natural human way is to describe its universality as stemming from an event of the historic past. Any form in which an emphasis upon this universality of sin can be put is exceedingly useful.

Yet most of the instructive force of the portrayal is lost when we insist on thinking of the events of Eden as simply the story of a great moral calamity of the past. In so doing, we find it easy to hide from our own responsibility behind an ancestral flaw, and to say, "Well, what can you expect from one so tainted as I?" This story becomes much more meaningful and fulfills its intended purpose much more effectively when we reverse it in the time-sequence of our thinking. Man's rebellion against God and the substitution of his will for that of God is not ancient history; it is daily practice. In 1914 Chancellor von Bethmann-Hollweg made a speech to the German Reichstag in which he said: "Gentlemen, we are now in a state of necessity, and necessity knows no law! Our troops have occupied Luxembourg, perhaps even have already entered Belgian territory. Gentlemen, this violates the rules of international law. . . . The injustice—I speak frankly—the injustice which we thus commit we will try to make good again as soon as our military goal has been achieved." Not many of us are so frank, but all of us have this same "necessity knows no law" attitude.

At a wedding rehearsal the best place to begin is at the end. That is, before starting the processional it is best for all members of the wedding party to take their places at the front of the church where they will be standing during the ceremony. Then, knowing the exact spot toward which they are moving, all the persons involved can later move confidently in the processional. The study of Genesis 3 is much like a wedding rehearsal in this respect. In a sense it is best understood after reading all the rest of the Bible first. This chapter is part of the total revelation that culminates in Christ. Because of Him, as we move farther and farther into the future, we move, not away from Eden, but toward it, through the events of the Fall to stand with redeemed mankind in order before God. The bliss of the early verses of the Garden of Eden story is, as it were, the diagram of our ultimate destination, like the wedding party standing before the altar. At the present we are in the situation of marching down the aisle. We are not in our ultimate position. We are prodigal children; but the picture of the Garden of Eden, the place of intimate, personal fellowship with God, is the diagram of the state toward which, through Christ, we are moving.

In the words of J. S. Whale: "The Fall is symbolism, necessary to the intellect, but inconceivable by the imagination. It involves no scientific description of absolute beginnings. Eden is on no map, and Adam's fall fits no historical calendar. Moses is not nearer to the Fall than we are because he lived three thousand years before our time. The Fall refers not to some datable aboriginal calamity in the historic past of humanity, but to a dimension of human experience which is always present— namely, that we who have been created for fellowship with God repudiate it continually; and that the whole of mankind does this along with us. Everyman is his own 'Adam,' and all men are solidarily 'Adam.' Thus, Paradise before the Fall . . . is not a period of history, but our 'memory' of a divinely intended quality of life, given to us along with our consciousness of guilt. . . . Man's tragic apostasy from God is not something which happened once for all a long time ago. It is true in every moment of existence." [13]

Instead, then, of yearning disconsolately for Paradise before the Fall, turn the picture around. Think of the Garden of Eden, not as a forever-lost perfection, but as a divinely promised goal that God wants you to attain and to be. Along with the sense of guilt that comes with wrongdoing is a corresponding consciousness of what you ought to be. That is part of God's taking the initiative for your salvation. In Christ the goal has already come. When we consent to our adoption as children of God, we wait for an inheritance whose details are unknown to us but whose essential and most glorious nature is that we shall be "like him." (I John 3:2.) "Thanks be unto God for his unspeakable gift." [14]

FOUR

The Tale of the City of Beginning

GENESIS 4

THOSE who would worry about where Cain got his wife are missing a much more major field of difficulty. The precise literary relation of this chapter to the ones that have gone before is very difficult to establish, though it apparently begins in logical enough fashion with the birth of children to Adam and Eve. Yet Cain and Abel are represented as offering sacrifices to God, whereas the last verse in the chapter says that it was only in the time of Enos (or Enosh), much later, that men "began . . . to call upon the name of the Lord." Moreover, Adam was sentenced to till the ground, but Abel, the son who is favorably portrayed, "was a keeper of sheep." Again, Cain's expressed fear that "every one that findeth me shall slay me" implies inhabitants of the earth who were not Cain's brethren. As a matter of fact, to a great extent this story seems to present in another form an account of the Fall and man's expulsion from Eden.

These inconsistencies give strong support to the opinion of those scholars who say that we have in these chapters a putting together of stories originally told separately from one another, each complete in itself and carrying its own message, and each retaining enough of its original form so that it does not harmonize in every detail with the other stories. The inspired nature of the total record is vividly emphasized by the way in which it utterly refuses to quibble about minor matters which mere men would exalt into major problems and moves piercingly and majestically forward in the delineation of the mighty acts of God. It is not the purpose of this narrator to write the history of the world or even the history of mankind. He is writing a history of redemption. We turn to this chapter, then, conscious that we are not just turning a page in a polished, integrated literary masterpiece, but that we are opening another revelation of man's eternal relationship to God.

The meaning of the term "knew" in the opening words of the chapter, "And Adam knew Eve his wife; and she conceived, and bare Cain," is perfectly obvious. But to use it here is more than a mere delicacy of expression. This is a usage which perfectly demonstrates the Hebrew conception of "knowledge." We met it in consideration of the "tree of the knowledge of good and evil." "Knowing," in Hebrew thought, is not primarily an academic or intellectual exercise. It involves active personal response to the person known. The sense of self-giving and surrender of the self is in it. In this sense sexual relationship is far more spiritual than it is physical. Far beyond being merely a means of procreation, it is the fullest, truest, and most satisfying kind of knowledge that exists. Conversely, the fact that procreation is a result of two people's "knowing" one another in a most intimate and profound way is a fact of tremendous significance in human life. Some researchers feel that they have grounds for believing that decided psychological tendencies are imparted to a child at the very time of conception.

The implication of active personal response must be understood in all passages where the Bible speaks of knowledge of God. Often the most intimate knowledge of God that Israel has is spoken of as Lover-loved or Husband-wife relationship; and when Israel is faithless she is denounced as a harlot. The message of Hosea is especially effective because he moves so readily from his own tragic experience as the husband of a faithless wife into the portrayal of God's flaunted but abiding love. Amos voices God's words to His people, "You only have I known of all the families of the earth." (Amos 3:2.) In both Old and New Testaments knowledge of God invariably carries with it the sense of entering into active personal relations with Him. The god who can be idly discussed with one's feet upon the desk is not the God of the Bible.

There is some intimation that Cain and Abel may have been twins in the phrase, "And she again bare his brother Abel." "In process of time it came to pass" that each brought an offering to God of the fruit of his labors. Nothing in the record here tells why "the Lord had respect unto Abel and to his offering: but unto Cain and to his offering he had not respect." The most helpful commentary is found in the Epistle to the Hebrews, where we are told that "by faith Abel offered unto God a more excellent sacrifice than Cain." (Hebrews 11:4.) The assumption must be that Abel offered a humble token of gratitude and adoration, while Cain offered his gift in the proud spirit of submitting proof of his skill and his works. In any event, Cain knew that his worship was unacceptable to God.

The Hebrew of the verses recounting Cain's conversation with God about the offering is not clear, but out of it a general paraphrase may be constructed: "Cain, why are you so angry? You have brought an offering that is not acceptable because you are not acceptable in your present proud and haughty spirit. But the remedy lies in yourself. You are not permanently barred from devotion. If you do well, you will be accepted, together with your offering. If you do not do well, the fault is not in Abel nor in anyone else, but in yourself. Like a wild beast, sin crouches at the door of your impetuous heart, ready to spring upon you; but you must control it."

Despite the warning, Cain brooded over his rejected offering, and his jealous anger smoldered hotter and hotter against his brother. Even so today we see bitter, jealous mockery and anger directed toward the righteous by the unrighteous, not because of any wrong done but simply because the unrighteous cannot bear to see the thing he truly longs for but has never attained. If he cannot have it, he will not allow anyone else to possess it. Oscar Wilde put it, "Yet each man kills the thing he loves." So in a flame of passion, "when they were in the field" away from any observers, "Cain rose up against Abel his brother, and slew him."

Two "firsts" appear in the record here. The first death in

the narrative takes place. As the full consciousness of what he had done began to dawn upon Cain, we may imagine him trying to rouse Abel, seeking to discover that his act of violence was not altogether final, that he still might turn time back, that he yet might revive the past that he had destroyed. But his efforts were fruitless. In an instant he had made for himself a new world in which he must reap the harvest of what he had sowed. After the first death in the narrative comes the first question addressed by man to God: "Am I my brother's keeper?" The question is really an attempted evasion of a question God has put to him: "Where is Abel thy brother?" This question Cain has answered with a lie: "I know not." The smoldering fire of self-will is flaring up higher. Adam and Eve readily confess their guilt; Cain stubbornly resists authority, lying as he does so. Then he sullenly questions his responsibility for his brother. Thus is depicted the spreading, infectious nature of sin, the setting of man's will against God's. Man's life is sacred, not because man is valuable in himself nor because his life is a tiny spark of the divine life, but because man is made in God's image and likeness. Men are valuable because God loves them, and in the revelation later to come in Christ each man becomes to the other "the brother for whom Christ died." No such idea is exhibited in Cain's attitude. No will but his own is considered. To be human is to be responsible, responsible to God and for one's brother; and Cain rejects that elemental human obligation.

The punishment pronounced upon Cain is twofold. First, "when thou tillest the ground, it shall not henceforth yield unto thee her strength." This is parallel to the earlier words in 3:17, "cursed is the ground for thy sake," and is another expression of the discernment that the mystery of evil reaches into all nature as well as all human life. The second part of the punishment is that Cain shall be "a fugitive and a vagabond" upon the earth. In response to the punishment there is still no indication of remorse on his part; there is only a vast self-pity: "My punishment is greater than I can bear. . . . every one that findeth me shall slay me."

In the face of such a spirit comes a demonstration of the "miracle and mystery" of grace. God will not let Cain go nor abandon him to his justly merited fate. Wherever Cain wanders, even far away from the acknowledged presence of God, he goes with a "mark" upon him "lest any finding him should kill him." This is not called such, but it is in actuality a covenant, made with sinful man. God cares not only for the victim, Abel, but also for the murderer, Cain. Just what the nature of the "mark" was can only be conjectured, but the mercy which prompted its bestowal is the significant fact. For future reference, however, note the words, "whosoever slayeth Cain, vengeance shall be taken on him sevenfold."

So Cain "went out from the presence of the Lord, and dwelt in the land of Nod ["wandering"], on the east of Eden." He made a new beginning. He begat a son, and he built a city; and to both he gave the name "Enoch," which means "initiation" or "beginning." The name is significant. It is not straining a point to read into it a whole attitude. That attitude was one of putting aside the past, the memories of a former home, a murder, and God. Here was to be a fresh beginning and a new line of the family established, not with former misdeeds forgiven, but with them forgotten. This was a city whose founder was reconciled to himself but not to God; but can reconciliation to one's self be complete without reconciliation toward God?

As the quality of a tree can be determined finally only by its fruit, so may the quality of a society be assessed. Cain set himself to cultivate out of the world the curse of his sinfulness, and in the fifth generation from him the fruit of his efforts may be most clearly seen. That fifth-generation descendant was Lamech. "And Lamech took unto him two wives: the name of the one was Adah, and the name of the other Zillah. And Adah bare Jabal: he was the father of such as dwell in tents, and of such as have cattle. And his brother's name was Jubal: he was the father of all such as handle the harp and organ. And Zillah, she also bare Tubal-cain, an instructor of every artificer in brass and iron: and the sister of Tubal-cain was Naamah."

Here is marvelous achievement! This is the picture of a highly developed society. Examine its components with care. Its foundation was scientific agriculture. Perhaps "scientific" might seem too ambitious a word to use, but the phrase "such as dwell in tents" indicates a revolutionary development. This was deliberate design to increase efficiency in agricultural pursuits. Instead of being tied to a fixed habitation, with a consequently limited area of grazing and watering, Jabal conceived the idea of moving his house with him, following the herds to better grazing lands, moving as often as necessary to provide for ever-increasing numbers. The idea was a simple and obvious one, but so are a great many of our most radical developments. Most of our conservation practices of today are applications of obvious principles which have been ignored for generations. The idea of growing trees as fast as they are cut or of returning to the soil of cultivated fields a major portion of the vegetable growth on them is simple but revolutionary as compared with former practices. Jabal, then, with his revolutionary introduction of migratory animal husbandry is the prototype of the astute agriculturist.

"And his brother's name was Jubal: he was the father of all such as handle the harp and pipe." (The King James Version has the word "organ" instead of "pipe." The organ is certainly the direct descendant of the simple pipe, but the reference to an instrument so complex as a pipe organ in these primitive surroundings is far less desirable than the more accurate word "pipe.") Jubal was the father of culture, the fine arts. The vast majority of our musical instruments are simply elaboration of the basic principles of physics which are demonstrated by the variations of tones produced by vibrating strings of varying lengths or variable columns of air in a pipe. This was a reaching beyond mere utility, beyond mere food and drink and shelter; Jubal led in the development of esthetic enjoyment, in the adornment of life with pleasures of the spirit.

The significant thing is that this was a planned and devised process. It was not just enjoyment of the song of a bird or the roaring of the wind in a tempest or its gentle sighing in an evening zephyr. "Here was the man who first made a piece of wood help him; who out of the commonest material of the physical world found for himself a means of expressing the most impalpable moods of his spirit. Once the idea was caught that matter inanimate as well as animate was man's servant and could do his finest work for him, Jabal and his brother Jubal would make rapid work between them. If the rude matter of the world could *sing* for them, what might it not do for them? They would see that there was a precision in machine-work which man's hand could not rival—a regularity which no nervous throb could throw out and no feeling interrupt . . ." [1] Jubal was the author of a veritable Industrial Revolution.

This Cain-descended society had still a third major component; it had technology: "And Zillah, she also bare Tubal-cain, a smith who devised brass and iron tools." [2] Tubal-cain shared his brother Jubal's genius for invention and an even more abundant handiness and practical faculty for embodying his ideas in material form. Civilization was emerging out of barbarism. "Here [the Tigris-Euphrates plain] without question the spark of civilization was kindled spontaneously for the first time anywhere on earth. . . . From the standpoint of science and invention [this] was more fruitful than any other era of human history prior to the age of Galileo and Newton. For it produced the wheel; it ushered in what is commonly known as the Bronze Age, and through the mysterious genius of the human mind it engendered arithmetic and writing." [3]

Thousands of years of research and experiment have developed the tools of Tubal-cain into machines and instruments so significant in the life and welfare of mankind that man has been defined by some as "a tool-using animal." The products of these tools have been so marvelous and have so bemused man that he might be defined today as "a tool-worshiping animal." The machine is a veritable god in our civilization, which, when worshiped by offering suitably costly sacrifices of devotion of life and skills, will supply every need and want of mankind. "Technology is my shepherd, I shall not want," is a paraphrase that is dangerously easy to believe.

A final gloss to this family portrait is in the words, "and the sister of Tubal-cain was Naamah." In the mere mention of her, all the more significant since feminine characters are seldom mentioned in the Old Testament genealogies, is a reminder of the strength of woman's influence in any society. It has been said that men have the making of civilization, but women have the making of men. Women largely determine the tone of a society. It is they who really make many of the decisions men think they make themselves. If documentation is needed, read the day's newspaper or magazine and note to which sex the advertisers make their appeal. No woman can renounce her influence; it is there for help or hurt. Later legend calls Naamah the mother of singing. Humming her lullabies, woman has quietly and thoroughly dominated civilization.

This, then, is the society Cain began. This, surely, is an enduring civilization. It gives every evidence of being a vigorous, progressive, healthy social system. Its features excite our admiration; here are a people who are making their mark in the world. Their society has beauty, it has power and resources, it has abundant promise of limitless development, it has an air of efficient productiveness. Though it is primitive by our present standards, it has in it the same features to which we point with pride in our Western civilization: scientific agriculture, culture, and technology. What more could be desired? Perhaps Cain succeeded in cultivating his ancient curse out of the world.

But wait! There is still to be considered a snatch of song. We have only one recorded utterance from the lips of Lamech, but like a mighty trumpet blast it startles us out of any complacency about the necessary components of a model society. Proudly surveying the achievements of his sons, Lamech sang a song, which George Adam Smith renders:

> "Adhah and Sillah, hear ye my voice,
> Lemekh's-wives, hearken my speech,
> For a man I slew for a wound to me,

And a youth for a blow to me.
If Cain avenges himself seven times,
Truly Lemekh seventy times and seven." [4]

It is not clear whether he meant he had actually killed a man or whether he was stating a hypothetical case. It makes no difference, for the character of his words is the same in either case. How did he greet all the progress and adornment of human life in the achievements of his sons? With an outburst of thanksgiving to God? With gratitude for the enrichment of man's life and the easing of man's burdens? With none of these, but rather with a savage exultation in the fresh power of vengeance and domination that was now available to him. This is a weird and terrible anticlimax to the magnificent story of progress. The first result of civilization was to equip hatred and to render revenge more deadly. That far-off song seems to mock us with a grotesque reflection of our own day, with the major portion of the budgets of the leading nations of the world going to the development of enormous armaments and with war serving as the greatest spur to further technological advances. Lamech's song is as stunning as the outbreak of an atrocity-filled war in a world made "safe for democracy."

There was one element, you see, the major element, left out of the society in which Lamech was glorying. That element was God. So his song reveals a strutting pride, a sadistic vindictiveness, a coarse and cruel selfishness—and utter godlessness. After his crime one slender thread still bound Cain to God: his acknowledged need of protection. He implored God for that and was granted his request. Lamech's attitude was different. "I can take care of my own protection," he boasted. "These good instruments devised by my sons furnish me with a means of defense many times more effective than Cain's protection. Only weaklings and backward peoples need God. I can improve on God. If Cain shall be avenged sevenfold, truly Lamech seventy and sevenfold. What my sons can make and my own right hand can do are enough for me." No doubt Jesus had in mind this boastful expression of a spirit diametrically opposed to His own when He answered Peter's question, "Lord, how oft shall my brother sin against me, and I forgive him? till seven times?" Jesus' reply was, "I say not unto thee, Until seven times: but, Until seventy times seven." (Matthew 18:21-22.)

This is what comes of finding enough in the world without God: cruel self-sufficiency and deadly hostility toward society. The very success of the pattern of life that had been established contributed to this arrogance of spirit. Such success is a stumbling block in life both to the religious and to the irreligious. "Fret not thyself because of evildoers," admonishes the psalmist. (Psalm 37:1.) Yet we do fret, because so often they prosper bountifully. The religious man fumes because the wicked man has a Midas' touch, and the unscrupulous scoundrel chuckles with pride over his achievements and grows more sure in his conviction that piety is irrelevant to real life. Our language pays tribute to this experience, for when we call something "worldly," we are acknowledging that it has success in the world. If that were not so, we would call it "other-worldly," something not adapted to this world. Lord Beaverbrook of England once said, "Money is nothing but the fruit of resolution and intellect applied to the affairs of the world. To an unshakeable resolution fortune will oppose no bar." In other words, if you set out for worldly success, there is no reason on earth, or out of it, why you should not get it. Piety is no substitute for brains and perseverance. Even Jesus remarked that "the children of this world are in their generation wiser than the children of light." (Luke 16:8.) The possibilities of the world are almost literally infinite; and there is hardly any desire, any ambition, any principle of living, to which it cannot afford some sort of support and satisfaction if you are persistent enough and clever enough and ruthless enough.

It takes a long view and a resolute examination of what we regard as "success" to keep our moral footing. But here our story may give some added help, for Lamech's song ends the tale of the City of Beginning. Abruptly and completely the story ends here. Those who know the art of storytelling say that a properly told tale needs no pointing out of its moral. Tell the story, and stop, they say, and the moral will make its own way. That seems to be the technique here, for never again in the pages of Scripture is this Lamech, or any of his children, mentioned. The name Lamech occurs again, as do many other Biblical names, in connection with other characters; but this Lamech is never again alluded to. The splendid society of the city of Enoch is completely dismissed from the record of the enduring events of man's history.

In violation of good storytelling technique we may dwell for a bit on the moral of the tale. For illustration, call to mind another culture known to us all. Germany, in unusual measure, possessed scientific agriculture, culture, and technology. Then along came a leader who cast aside the concept of the sovereignty of God. The skills of Germany were devoted to equipping hatred and rendering revenge more deadly. And the story is the same from Enoch to Berlin: oblivion lies that way.

With the abrupt ending of the story of the line of Cain in Lamech, the record returns to Adam and Eve and to the birth of a third son, Seth. Then, in the first part of chapter 5, there is a sort of thumb-nail recapitulation of the creation story and a continuation of the genealogy from Adam and Eve through Seth as though Cain and Abel had not existed. In the fifth generation from Seth, roughly contemporary with Lamech and his sons, the monotony of the record of births and deaths is broken by the words, "And Enoch [this is another Enoch than the one who descended from Cain] walked with God: and he was not; for God took him." To "walk with God" is an expression used to denote perfect fellowship with God and implies a man of especially holy and righteous life. So evident was this close relationship with God that when Enoch disappeared one day, the logical explanation was that "God took him." It is the family line of this godly man that history follows. It always does. History belongs to them.

The story is told. May its moral be heeded: an enduring society cannot be built in forgetfulness of God.

FIVE

The Wages of Sin

GENESIS 5-9

THE long genealogy of chapter 5 is not meant to furnish an accurate timetable of events. All the genealogies of the Bible are worthy of more study than they usually enlist, for they ordinarily have more significance than a mere listing of names. This one is meant, in part, to imply the passage of many years of time. For another thing, it does not mention Cain and Abel but proceeds straight from Adam through Seth to succeeding generations. Thus our hopes are aroused that the outbreak of sin in Cain and its obscene fruitage in the vindictive Lamech is a forever past bit of ugliness. Like a raging epidemic the infection of sin had spread from the seemingly innocuous eating of forbidden fruit on to a sullen son and then to his family. But perhaps, also, the epidemic has run its unpredictable course. Here is an apparently disease-resistant strain through Seth. Does the line not contain one so signally righteous as to have it said of him that he "walked with God"? Then abruptly we find ourselves reading a record of gross evil and corruption in the story of Noah and the Flood. Once again we are face to face with the raw ugliness of rampant evil.

The prelude to that story is a strange section of four verses at the beginning of chapter 6 of Genesis. This bears little relation to what goes before and after it, so far as historical record is concerned; but it does embody an insight that is most appropriate as an introduction to the flood story. The purpose of it seems to be an effort to account for the abnormal wickedness about to be mentioned by tracing its origin to abnormal marriages between heavenly and earthly creatures. "The sons of God" are met again in Job 1:6 when they "came to present themselves before the Lord, and Satan came also among them." And when Peter and Jude mention the "fall" of certain angels, "which kept not their first estate, but left their own habitation," [1] perhaps they are referring to this story.

This fragmentary account is certainly very much akin to stories in pagan mythology about abnormal relations between gods and humans, and the giant offspring of those relations, such as the Greek Titans. Perhaps, though, the pagan myths are reflections of a haunting truth which is also the insight incorporated in this story and which makes it a fitting prelude to this portion of the Biblical record. This is part of the Bible's realistic, accurate portrayal of sin as a grievously serious and deadly thing. The Fall is not just a minor human misadventure; it is cosmic in its scope, for "the whole creation groaneth and travaileth in pain together until now." [2] Evil is a sinister cosmic reality, not just a defect of human nature that can be patched up as good as new by the ministrations of education, sociology, politics, and psychology. Evil exists outside and beyond human nature, though its manifestations are most apparent when human nature becomes its tool and instrument. Because man's nature does become corrupted by this sinister demonic power, his days upon earth are numbered: "his days shall be an hundred and twenty years," a reflection of the thought that imperfection cannot be eternal, as expressed in Genesis 3: ". . . lest he put forth his hand, and take also of the tree of life, and eat, and live for ever: therefore the Lord God sent him forth from the garden of Eden . . ."

As we continue from this prelude into the story of the flood, we notice at once the length of it. The account occupies as many pages as the twice-told story of creation and the story of the Garden of Eden combined. There may be special significance to this relative length, but just what it may be is not readily apparent. One possible reason is that a different method of compilation of material is used here. Previously in the narrative, sections of two different stories have been placed together consecutively; in the account of the flood the two sources are woven into a single account. Another reason may be that a very large amount of source material was available. In the traditions of primitive peoples as far separated as Australia, Eastern Asia, Africa, and North America are found legends of a great flood. The Babylonian story is closely parallel to that of Genesis, and recent archaeological findings in Mesopotamia give strong evidence of a vast inundation of that area since the time of human habitation. All of this, however, has only minor importance with reference to the Genesis account. It is not told for the purpose of establishing the historicity of Noah nor to authenticate a legend about a great flood. Its sole purpose is to present a magnificent conception of the awe-fulness of God's judgment and the wonderful quality of His mercy.

The great number of details supplied here has given rise to endless speculation and calculation. As described, the ark was about 450 feet in length, 75 feet in width, and 45 feet in height. The term "ark" is used to denote a vessel without means of propulsion. It was simply a vast floating box, nearly half the length of the *Queen Elizabeth* and more than half as wide. Its proportions, according to some nautical calculators, made it perfect as a freight-carrying vessel. Moreover, another set of calculations estimated that 6,666 pairs of animals and birds could have been stowed away in one tenth of the capacity of the Ark, leaving the other nine tenths for provisions. But our purpose in examining this story is not to get a lesson in shipbuilding. We are looking at an item in the moral history of mankind.

We find, then, a picture of the persistent deadliness of sin. "And God saw that the wickedness of man was great in the earth, and that every imagination of the thoughts of his heart was only evil continually. . . . The earth also was corrupt before God, and the earth was filled with violence. And God looked upon the earth, and, behold, it was corrupt; for all flesh had corrupted his way upon the earth." [3] Even in the English translation the language is cumulative, piling adjective upon adjective to suggest repulsive sordidness on a mass scale. The result was catastrophe.

Physically speaking, mankind inhabits a thin crust of earth, dependent for his sustenance on the ten or twelve inches of topsoil, breathing from a thin layer of atmosphere, his climate so delicately balanced by the distance of the earth from the sun and by the composition of the air above him that a very few degrees variation in the average temperature could annihilate him. But man also lives in a morally delicately balanced world. Even more sensitive than his physical being to his surroundings is his spiritual nature in relation to its environment. Let him go one hundred per cent into evil, and he will be so far out of harmony with the universe that it will rise up and annihilate him. It was a force of nature which annihilated wicked man in this story, and that fact stands as a giant symbol of the truth that a universe created by a righteous God has woven into every atom of its being a harmony toward righteousness and a hostility toward evil.

This relationship between morality and the physical world is a fertile field for thought. Just how much, if any, correlation is there between nature and morality? Some areas of our country have changed drastically in appearance, climate, and the subtle, unsuspected relationships the naturalists call "ecology." In one such area, a rancher, looking across acres of barren, rocky pasture, said, "My father said that when he came here, you could not find a rock on the surface of the ground, and the grass was stirrup-high to a horseman." Pointing to distant thick brush beneath which no grass, even the surviving short varieties, could grow, he continued, "And a man could climb a windmill tower and see every head of stock in the pasture. There was no brush to hide them and to choke out the grass." But more than those changes had taken place. The deer were much smaller; the wild turkeys were scarce; wild animals that once were abundant had vanished, and new species, formerly unknown, were increasing in numbers. The rivers dried up quickly in dry weather and flooded destructively when rains came. Game fish became scarce and "rough" fish thrived because of the irregular water level. The whole country had undergone vast changes in one generation. The reason? Relentless overstocking of the land, a form of greed caused by desire or necessity to wring the last dollar of profit out of the land, regardless of the long-range effect.

This is not the pointing of an accusing finger at one group of people as sinners above all others. It is an illustration of a guilt we all share. But it raises the question that if such a clear connection exists between the physical aspects of a land and one apparently unrelated moral principle, is it not entirely possible that there may be a deeper and more subtle connection between man's righteousness and such things as earthquakes, tornadoes, drought, and a whole list of natural phenomena? Admittedly this sounds very farfetched, but we have come to see in recent years that the line between material and spiritual is not nearly so sharply drawn as we once thought.

Such a suggestion certainly should not be taken as even remotely hinting at the idea that persons suffering from a natural catastrophe are thereby clearly labeled as being unusually wicked. Jesus' remarks in Luke 13 about the relative guiltlessness of those "upon whom the tower in Siloam fell" should be corrective enough for any such thought. The suggestion is that the disharmony produced by sin is vastly more far-reaching than we have yet been able, or willing, to comprehend. Sin is catastrophe of the first magnitude, and the human eye has not seen to the limits of its poisonous reaches. The Hebrew prophets are not at all averse to attributing various natural plagues to the wickedness of the people, and Isaiah draws a glowing picture of natural harmony when "the earth shall be full of the knowledge of the Lord, as the waters cover the sea." Then "the wolf also shall dwell with the lamb, and the leopard shall lie down with the kid; and the calf and the young lion and the fatling together; and a little child shall lead them. And the cow and the bear shall feed; their young ones shall lie down together: and the lion shall eat straw like the ox. And the sucking child shall play on the hole of the asp, and the weaned child shall put his hand on the adder's den. They shall not hurt nor destroy in all my holy mountain." [4]

But if this story has warning in it, it also carries a message of vast reassurance. God is faithful in preserving all that we commit to Him. Through the long years when the ark was being built Noah must have suffered almost intolerable ridicule, and he had nothing but his faith to sustain him. As such he becomes the type and symbol of all who trust and obey God in every age. Peter likens the ark to baptism into the Church.[5] There is a way of putting our trust in God so that an old life and an old world perish, and we walk out into a new world, purged of its evil allure, radiant with the freshness of God.

If the inspired writer of these stories had been more interested in composing a polished literary masterpiece than in conveying moral and spiritual truths, he would have reconciled some apparent discrepancies. In one place two of every kind of living creature are said to have been taken into the ark, while in another place seven of the "clean beasts" are said to have been taken. This presupposes a designation of ritually "clean" and "unclean" animals which did not take place until much later in Hebrew history. There is variation also in comment on the amount of time the flood lasted. One statement has the waters "prevail" for 150 days and remain on the earth for a year and eleven days altogether. In another place the waters "increase" forty days and forty nights, and then disappear after three weeks, thus remaining on the earth for sixty-one days altogether. These are places where the two sources used by the writer were not identical, and instead of harmonizing them, he simply sets them down side by side to be sure not to obliterate any peculiarly valuable bit of insight each may bear.

Some significant advances in man's relationship to God are indicated in the flood story. The nature of God could not be revealed fully to man in one sudden illumination. God's power could be understood, at least to some extent, in observing the might of the physical forces of nature and in seeing them as the works of God. But His attributes of justice and goodness and mercy had to come from watching how He acted in history, how with unchanging consistency He opposed evil, blessed righteousness, and showed mercy "unto thousands . . . that love me, and keep my commandments." (Exodus 20:6.) Moreover, man's position of intimate fellowship with God and of being a laborer "together with God" [6] had been so obscured by his rebellious will that God continually had to take the initiative, as He still does, to woo man back to that high position.

One advance in being a laborer together with God may be noted by observing that Noah is not only the recipient of God's saving grace but is also the agent of it to save from destruction the members of his family and the animals of the earth. God steps back out of the picture a degree, so to speak, entrusting to Noah, as His responsible agent, the carrying out of His purposes. Yet notice how even here there is the demand for obedience. Noah's decision is basically the same as that which confronted Adam and Eve: obedience or disobedience. When there is no sign of impending catastrophe, Noah must believe God implicitly. When the months grow long, the labor arduous and apparently ridiculous; when the mockery of the scoffers becomes almost unbearable, Noah must constantly be resolute to do God's will and not his own. "And Noah did according unto all that the Lord commanded him." Thus simply is recorded the victory of Noah over pride and self-will, and the obedience by which he becomes the agent of God's saving purpose.

A fresh picture of man's relationship to God in grace is given here. When the flood subsides, Noah builds an altar and offers sacrifices to God. Thus he indicates that he purposes to continue the obedience he first displayed in building and entering the ark. God, on His side, accepts man for what he has become. By now evil has become innate in man, "for the imagination of man's heart is evil from his youth." [7] But this evil will not be punished to the full. Even if it should come to pass again that "all flesh had corrupted his way upon the earth," [8] God will not again bring total ruin upon the earth. Instead, the world in which man shall live will be settled and reliable: "While the earth remaineth, seedtime and harvest, and cold and heat, and summer and winter, and day and night shall not cease." This is the first step in God's self-denial for the sake of mankind, which reaches its full expression when the Son of God "made himself of no reputation, and took upon him the form of a servant, and was made in the likeness of men." (Philippians 2:7.)

The expression of this grace is embodied in a new, explicit form. It centers around the word "covenant." This word, which from this time on becomes a characteristic word of the Old Testament record, appears for the first time in the Bible in God's words to Noah in Genesis 6:18. True, the conditions of a covenant were present in the Garden of Eden and in Cain's banishment, but the covenant idea is brought to the forefront in God's dealings with Noah. The thought of a covenant between God and man is a relationship distinctive of and fundamental in Biblical religion. "It implies a *binding* of two parties, a linking together of two dissimilar or hitherto unrelated persons or groups (there could be no covenants between brethren). Thus the distinction is retained between God and man, while at the same time their binding together is emphasized. . . . God *binds* Himself to His people, but this is a voluntary act of God's grace: He had no obligations towards them and they had no claim upon Him. The parties to the covenant are not equals; it is of the infinite grace and mercy of God that He binds Himself in a covenant which He will not break." [9]

In contrast with some later covenants which were made with the nation or a remnant of it, this covenant with Noah is made "between me and you and every living creature that is with you, for perpetual generations." Six times within eight verses this inclusive declaration is made. The divine claim of lordship over all, established in creation, is thus reiterated and renewed. Without the constant covenanted care and protection of God, whether men recognize the fact or not, human life could not continue for an instant. No man is cut off from the knowledge of God, save by his own depravity; yet despite his depravity, no man is beyond the care and loving-kindness of God.

Out of this covenant relationship between God and man comes the foundation of society and government, for it is in the idea of man as a creature who has the capacity for covenanting with God that the unimaginable dignity of the "image of God" in man becomes most apparent. It is God's nature, revealed here by His own initiative, to enter into covenant with man. Man reflects that image in his capacity for covenant-sharing. He is, then, made for society, for the making and keeping of obligations both to God and to his fellows. He is made for reciprocity. His primary invitation is into a covenant relationship with God. Noah, standing as the representative of man, is invited into that relationship as the distinctive creature among all others, as the one capable of responding and thus becoming an agent for the working of the covenant blessings to all other created things.

In the spirit of this primal dignity of man in the covenant-status into which God has invited him, Noah is granted a responsibility which is the beginning of social organization and government. "Whoso sheddeth man's blood, by man shall his blood be shed." When Cain slew Abel, his punishment was inflicted directly by God. In the covenant with Noah, God delegates responsibility. It is in a most elemental matter, the protection of human life against the crime of murder, but this is the same crime in which God had previously been the direct agent of judgment. So here is an expansion of man's commission to "have dominion" into the realm of self-government through social processes.

Yet, even as that is done, the underlying principle is restated: "for in the image of God made he man." The implications of that are vast and of primary importance. Politically it implies that when man governs man in such a way that the covenant-sharing "image of God" in him is honored and aided and respected, the authority of both man and God is in the law, and "the powers that be are ordained of God." (Romans 13:1.) But when man governs man in such a way as to stifle and warp and ignore that image of God, the authority of God is withdrawn, and it becomes right for the oppressed to rebel and to "obey God rather than men." (Acts 5:29.) A careless, shallow, hasty decision on such a matter is dangerous and could lead to an anarchy in which "every man did that which was right in his own eyes." (Judges 17:6.) But deeply and prayerfully considered, it becomes the foundation of political liberty. In another realm it underscores the statement of Father Charles Pridgeon, Principal of the Catholic Workers' College, Oxford University, who has said in defense of voluntary unionism, "Let the unions remember that the right to work comes from God, not from men." With the establishment of the covenant with Noah, man's relationship with God was put on a higher plane than mere conformity to natural law. What was *right* became not what was required for harmonious relation to the natural world, but what the covenant required.

This is a major step in man's spiritual history. It holds forth to man his covenant-sharing status, and it also retains the vivid Hebrew insight of man's relation to God as a living, responsive, father-son relationship. The token of the covenant is the rainbow in the sky. The Hebrew word for war-bow is the same as that for rainbow. God has laid aside His wrath, hung up His war-bow in the heavens as a perpetual symbol of His covenant of mercy. And yet, strikingly, not one word is said here of man's obligation. The covenant is unconditional; no requirement is made upon man. Instead, man is left to look upon the mercy of God, whose absolute sovereignty is unquestionable, and, in free response, to love God and to listen for His leading voice. Man's part of the covenant is not summed up in a formal code of behavior. Man is to live in a daily fellowship so close that he will hear and respond to a voice whispering in his ear, "This is the way, walk ye in it." (Isaiah 30:21.) Out of His free mercy God blazons across the sky the symbol of His obligation in the covenant. Man is invited into that mercy to share a continual, growing obedience to God as his part of covenant-sharing.

The story of Noah could have had a much happier ending if, like a scene on a movie screen, the picture had ended in the beautiful radiance of the rainbow. Instead, it fades from a scene of beauty into one of sordidness where Noah lies naked in his tent, drunk with wine made from grapes grown by his own labors. Throughout the Old Testament to be naked is a sign of

disgrace and humiliation, and to see, even accidentally, the nakedness of one's father is to bring shame and disgrace upon oneself.
The picture, then, is one of a man who had faced a whole world
of opposition without quailing, falling into abject and repellent
degradation. The Biblical heroes are not plaster saints, and the
record is very honest in speaking of their flesh-and-blood faults.
Some extensive moralizing could be done upon the subject of
Noah's fall, but that is beside our major concern here.

Shem and Japheth treat the situation with approved Hebrew
delicacy. Ham makes his father's ignominy the subject of coarse
jest. As a consequence, Noah pronounces a curse upon, not Ham,
but upon the son of Ham, Canaan. In Hebrew thought a father's
blessing or curse was no mere wish or petition; it was regarded as
having a self-fulfilling potency that determined the future. These
three sons of Noah were the fathers of the three great families of
mankind into which the Hebrews divided the inhabited world.
Shem, from which derives the name Semite, was the father of
the Hebrews themselves. Japheth was the father of the Gentiles.
Ham was the father of the Egyptians, Ethiopians, and Abyssin-
ians; but, more specifically, his son Canaan was the father of the
Canaanite inhabitants of Palestine whom the invading Hebrews
conquered and among whom they lived.

Canaanite worship was full of religious orgies of drunkenness
practiced in the worship of fertility gods. This sensuous worship was a constant temptation to the Hebrews and was also part
of their general estimation of the Canaanites as an inferior people.
The other Hamitic people, such as the Egyptians, were not regarded as inferiors in the same despised way that the Canaanites
were. The Canaanites literally suffered the curse pronounced
upon their ancestor by becoming bondservants to the Hebrews
during the reign of Solomon.

There are those who would make the curse upon Canaan a
justification for regarding the traditional descendants of Ham as
inferiors and as even justifying the subjection of those people
into slavery. The last twelve verses of Genesis 9, which include
the voicing of Noah's curse, contain just about as many dif-

ficulties and complexities as any passage of the same length in the
Old Testament, but they do not contain any justification of race
prejudice. It is noteworthy, though, that the first Biblical mention of ethnological divisions of mankind prompts us to begin
thinking of "superior" and "inferior" peoples. Previously mentioned divisions of men have been on the basis of trade or handi-
craft, as with Cain and Abel, and Jabal, Jubal, and Tubal-cain.
As soon as divisions on the basis of tribal families or nations are
mentioned, our pride goes to work to try to establish others as
being "inferior" to us.

The illogical cursing of a son, Canaan, for the coarse lack of
filial piety on the part of his father, Ham, should make us look at
the pre-eminent thing for which Canaan stood in Hebrew thinking. Devout Hebrews looked with horror upon the Canaanites
because of the gross sexual aspect of their religion. The worship
of Jehovah, they saw, could have nothing in common with "the
frenzied intoxication and exhibitionism of the Baal-cults." [10] The
curse upon Canaan, then, seems properly to be taken as a curse,
not upon an individual or race as such, but upon a culture which
exalts sensuous immorality.

If we heed the advice of Harvard sociologist Pitirim A.
Sorokin in a recent book entitled *The American Sex Revolution,*
we shall take this curse seriously and apply it currently. He is
of the opinion that our civilization has become so preoccupied
with sex that it now "oozes from all the pores of American
life." He points out that in its early stages Communism pro-
moted the utmost sexual freedom in Russia, but later reversed itself and enforced a strict code of sexual morality. One of the
lessons he draws from history is that sexual license is a very
effective tool for destroying a civilization, but a new civilization
cannot be created without sexual restraint. In sociological history he sees a close parallel between the sex habits of ancient
Egypt, Greece, and Rome during their decadence and the present sex revolution in America.

In that view of our modern situation the story of Noah's
downfall becomes very pertinent and can be turned into a highly

instructive parable for our own day and nation. Indeed, such usage of it almost certainly was made by the ancient Hebrews, Noah representing those who fell victim to the licentious Baal religion of the Canaanites. Transposed into a modern setting, Noah may represent a strong, clean people, our own or any other nation, blessed by God yet still full of all human frailties, brought low by succumbing to the constant lure of immorality. The curse upon Canaan is a denunciation of all who gloat over and abet the furtherance of such immorality, all those who pander to the debasing of essentially good and wholesome instincts, all those who prey selfishly for gain upon their fellow man's own selfish tendency to pervert everything to his own self-gratification. All those who look upon their fellows' weaknesses with naught but amusement and an eye to personal advantage, and who feel no strong compulsion to cover the shame and to aid in restoration of a lost dignity, are guilty of the callous selfishness of Ham. They become the propagators of a people like Canaan and his descendants, who glory in and even deify lust. Paul characterizes such persons in the first chapter of Romans as those "who changed the truth of God into a lie, and worshipped and served the creature more than the Creator . . . who knowing the judgment of God, that they which commit such things are worthy of death, not only do the same, but have pleasure in them that do them."

As we have already observed, the flood story would be much more lovely if it could close in the glowing radiance of the rainbow; but it would be less realistic if it ended there. The over-arching mercy of God, symbolized by that bow, has an even deeper meaning when we remember that it shines in the sky for Canaan as well as for the children of Shem and Japheth. The order of nature is now a corrupted order, but it is still God's. Except for God's mercy man's corrupted will would annihilate him, yet the earlier command is repeated, "Be fruitful, and multiply, and replenish the earth." [11] This is no second Paradise; all the descendants of Noah must struggle for existence with a nature and in a world tainted and marred by evil. Nevertheless, "the everlasting God, the Lord, the Creator of the ends of the earth, fainteth not, neither is weary." (Isaiah 40:28.)

SIX

Pride Goeth Before a Fall

GENESIS 10 AND 11

ONE more story, that of the Tower of Babel, remains to be considered in the pre-Abrahamic chapters of Genesis. The natural inclination is to skip directly to it in reading, thus omitting the tedium of the genealogy which fills all of Genesis 10. But there is more to this list of names than tedium, and further consideration given to it may add weight to what was said at the beginning of the previous chapter about the significance of Biblical genealogies.

The names given here, with one exception, are eponymous; that is, in a manner very common in the ancient world, each nation or tribe is regarded as descended from an ancestor whose name it bears; for example, Romulus and the Romans. The apparent exception to this usage of names is Nimrod, who is characterized as "a mighty one in the earth . . . a mighty hunter before the Lord." Even he is a person with wider than individual significance, for his character is exactly that of the warrior-huntsman-king of the Babylonian-Assyrian type. Babylonia and Assyria, with their mighty empires, fascinated and impressed the Hebrews long before they became imminent threats. So here is a slight but significant bit of special attention given to the prototype of the ruthless, powerful, world-dominating despots who brought Babylonia and Assyria to the zenith of worldly power.

This genealogy is couched in ethnological terms, but it is in fact largely geographical. Roughly speaking, it assigns the peoples of the north and west as descendants of Japheth, those of the south as descendants of Ham, and those of the east as descendants of Shem. While it has little or no scientific value from the standpoint of ethnology, there are two remarkable things about it. One is a surprising knowledge of the inhabited world. The peoples named were ancient inhabitants of lands from modern Spain or Corsica (Tarshish) to southern Russia (Gomer) to eastern Mesopotamia (Elam) to southernmost Arabia (Sheba, Havilah) to Ethiopia (Cush).

The other remarkable feature, the most important aspect of the genealogy, is its profound conception of God as Lord of all the earth and of all the nations upon it. This is sometimes regarded as being a new revelation that came through the late Hebrew prophets. In actuality they were re-emphasizing a truth that had become obscured, but which had been an item of Hebrew faith from as early as the compilation of this genealogy. The writer is setting forth the conviction that the history of Israel is no human accident, but that from the beginning it is shaped by the sovereign, purposeful will of God. God's purpose embraces all the nations, yet out of humanity in general God selects a people to be the instrument of His purpose of redemption. Thus, having swept over the whole roster of nations, the writer turns, after the Babel story, to resume a detailed following of the genealogy of Shem, narrowing the focus smaller and smaller until there stands sharply in the foreground the lone figure of that man of destiny, Abraham. This is tremendous drama. For any people thus to see and to hold the faith that God has selected them, out of all the nations of the earth, for an immortal destiny is to lift their national life to an exalted level. True, that lofty belief is capable of becoming distorted and narrow and selfish, but rightly conceived, it is power that can outlast any persecution.

Into the midst of this genealogical world-view the story of the Tower of Babel comes very fittingly, for it speaks of the diversity of peoples and tongues on the earth. In so doing it becomes an additional commentary upon the phrase used regarding each of the three major lines of descent: "after their tongues, in their countries, and in their nations." [1] Before looking at it, let us review again its background. The firstborn son of Adam and Eve was Cain. It would be most logical to assume that the line of history would follow him, the eldest son in the family. But a perversity of character caused him to kill his brother, Abel, in a fit of jealous rage. As we followed the development of his line of the human race, we saw it flourish in the worldly prosperity and promise of his descendant, Lamech, and then disappear from the record to the accompaniment of a vengeful, savage song of exultation over the fresh powers of vengeance made available by advanced technology.

Hopefully, then, the record turned back to the family line of Seth, another son of Adam and Eve. A fresh start was taken, and the record sounded very promising until we came to the picture of corruption and degeneracy at the time of Noah. The cataclysm of the flood exterminated all but Noah and his family within the ark, so once again there was a fresh start. Noah was described as being "a just man . . . upright," [2] one who "walked with God." In Cain was one start, and Cain succumbed to an innate flaw of human nature. In Seth was a fresh start, but the old evil cropped up again. In Noah, a strong, virtuous character despite his gross fall, yet another start was made in a world washed clean of outside evil. But in the story of the Tower of Babel we come up against the fact of evil again. We must remember that, according to the background painted for us in the record, the evil confronted in this story came from inside Noah and his descendants. The environment was purged; there was no excuse there, a favorite refuge for most of us. Adam used it: "The woman whom thou gavest to be with me, she gave me of the tree, and I did eat." He laid the blame upon outward circumstances, but the crucial point came after the last conjunction of his reply: "She gave me of the tree, and . . . " The sentence did not have to end as it did. An inward decision determined the conclusion of that sentence. His acquiescence came from within, from an act of his own will. From that same inward perversity of will came the evil that flourished after Noah.

It is as if the Biblical record is walking thoroughly around this great, tragic fact of sin, viewing it from every angle, trying to portray an opportunity given again and again to mankind to mend its ways, with each opportunity resulting in futility. The intended purpose seems to be to show that sin is something so persistently tenacious in the nature of man that all the skill and wisdom of man cannot eradicate it. Far from being a temporary handicap of unsophisticated man, far from being an inconsequential blemish that can be lightly sponged away by a few platitudes or a little more education, it is so deeply ingrained in the nature of man that nothing short of a new creation by the Creator Himself, changing the innermost nature of man, can save him.

As part of that procedure we have now to consider the story of the Tower of Babel. It is very simple and brief, told in the King James Version in two hundred and thirty-five words. It recounts that men in their migrations came upon what is still a fantastically fertile plain somewhere in the Tigris-Euphrates valley. There they settled down to build a city. So deep and rich was the soil that they did not have stones for building purposes. They used sun-dried bricks set in place with pitch for mortar. Architecturally the city was to be dominated by a tower, which they, in extravagant enthusiasm, said would reach "unto heaven." Then, in the very human way these stories have of speaking of God, God is pictured as coming down inquiringly from heaven to see what all the noise and bustle is about. What He saw troubled Him deeply. "Behold," He said, "the people is one, and they have all one language; and this they begin to do: and now nothing will be restrained from them, which they have imagined to do. Go to, let us go down, and there confound their language, that they may not understand one another's speech." So He scattered them abroad upon the face of the earth, and the name of the place was called Babel, which means "gate of God," but which by a play on words suggests the similar-sounding Hebrew verb "*balal*," meaning "to mix or confuse."

The name Babel is translated Babylon in all other places where it is mentioned in the Old Testament. Numerous pyramid-shaped towers, called ziggurats, with a shrine at the top were famous features of the Babylonian landscape. These were very impressive to the predominately rural Hebrews, and to them such structures would carry the appearance of human presumption and of vast conceit in human achievement. This is perhaps one detail of the total reason why throughout the Bible Babylon is used as the symbol of human corruption and megalomania. Perhaps, then, various writers are correct in saying that the splendid ziggurat Nebuchadnezzar built as one of the wonders of his fabulous city of Babylon inspired the "legend" of the Tower of Babel. The same writers also chronicle at length the desolation that was the ultimate fate of this grandiose display of human pride.

"Today all that remains of the splendor of the ancient cities of the plain subsists in cuneiform tablets and half-buried ruins that rise mutely from the dust-swept empty landscape. Of these ruins none is more starkly eloquent of the ravages of time and mankind than the desolate mound which marks the site of the once-glorious city of Ur. Where the pyramids of Egypt and the Parthenon of Athens flourish now as tourist centers, visited by thousands of sightseers each year, the remains of Ur stand silent in the wastes of the Iraqi desert.

"The once mighty ziggurat, eroded by wind and time, looms above a glaring wasteland. Around it the stark Iraqi plain extends in all directions, level and unbroken save by the distant mound of the Sumerian city of Eridu, lidded by the pale hemisphere of the sky. To the northeast the Euphrates weaves a lazy, green thread in its modern course. South of the ziggurat the ancient city sprawls—a desolation of roofless houses whose walls still define narrow, curving streets. But now the main inhabitants of Ur are snakes, birds and wolves which, seeking shade and shelter from the scorching sun, lurk hungrily amid the ruins and in the cool vaults of the surrounding tombs." [3]

What event prompted the Tower of Babel story is of no consequence whatever in comparison with what it teaches. It is another enlightening chronicle of the encounter of sinful humanity with the God of righteousness. It delineates another aspect of man's sinful will in its rebellion against God. It is a picture of human nature so intertwined with good and evil that man's noblest aspirations and achievements become the source of his defiance of God and oppression of his neighbor.

Some notice must be given to an attribute of God revealed here. It is that attribute later expressed in the second commandment, "I the Lord thy God am a jealous God." The modern mind has little patience with the idea of a jealous God. "It either does not believe in God at all, or the God of its faith is so very kind and fatherly as to be really grandmotherly." [4] Some time ago Life Magazine published pictures of the magnificent Michelangelo frescoes in the Sistine Chapel. The editor made a comment of praise for the majesty of the stern face of God in the creation scene. Numerous letters were received protesting that praise. The artist was wrong, said they; the face of God should be soft and gentle and kindly. True enough, there is that aspect of God; but since when do we have the right to assume that that is His *only* aspect? Since when do we, who cannot even abide one another and live harmoniously together, assume that God can look upon our rebellious wickedness and smile indulgently? The "jealousy" of God is a very vital one of His attributes.

However, we are prone to define the term with too much coloration from our human pride. God should not be thought of here as jealously preventing the progress of mankind to preserve His own supremacy. That is man's kind of jealousy. God's jealousy is redemptive, always concerned with man's blessing. The picture is that of God in His wisdom checking the presumptuous ambitions of men which are leading men away from their God-appointed destiny. There is a "God-shaped blank" in the human heart that only the Creator can fill, and His stern anger is set against any turning toward a pretender to that place, not because He is worried about His pre-eminence, but because a man with that counterfeit built into his life is less than whole.

Superficially the Tower of Babel story seems to be concerned with the origin of the diversity of languages upon earth, but a moment's reflection is enough to recognize the fact that confusion of tongues is not the center of this picture; sin is. We have here a further description both of what sin is and of what its consequences are. The sin at Babel is not the gross corruption and impure violence implied in the story of the flood. This is sophisticated, cultured sin. If all the sins to which man is subject could be classified as "the lust of the flesh, and the lust of the eyes," we might believe that what we call sin is just an evolutionary overhang, coming from our animal ancestry and certain to be outgrown in time. But John's classification of sins adds "the pride of life." (I John 2:16.) This is "the central, typical, fatal sin" of man, to use the phrasing of J. S. Whale. This sin of pride and self-sufficiency is in a different category entirely from the fundamental instinct of the animal world, the will to survive. This is a selfish will to power, man's proud unwillingness to accept the absolute authority and claim of God in whose image he has been made.

God's command to man in the beginning was that he should go in delegated authority to "be fruitful, and multiply, and replenish the earth, and subdue it." Man's response at Babel was, "Go to, let *us* build *us* a city and a tower, whose top may reach unto heaven; and let *us* make *us* a name, lest *we* be scattered abroad upon the face of the whole earth." There is a clear substitution of their will for God's will, haughty pride taking the place of obedience. The early Hebrews had no belief in a truly personal survival of death, and the way to become "immortal" was to leave behind a "name" in the form of fame, reputation, renown. The aim of Babel was to set up for glorification and eternal remembrance the "name" of man and not of God, to whom alone praise and glory properly belong.

Man continually builds his Towers of Babel. He is a truly wonderful creature, imprisoned in time and space, but touching the fringes of the eternal. His achievements are solid, and his towers of the spirit and of the material are high; but he constantly succumbs to the taint of pride within him and suffers the illusion that his towers reach higher than they do. "Man is mortal. That is his fate. Man pretends not to be mortal. That is his sin. . . . Human pride is greatest when it is based upon solid achieve-

ments; but the achievements are never great enough to justify
its pretensions. . . . In every Tower of Babel the foundation is
more honest than the pinnacle." [5]

All up and down the scale of magnitude this human trait
asserts itself. Man continually persuades himself that his truth is
the truth. Many a minister, striving with consecrated devotion
to lead his flock into deeper righteousness, trembles before his
most fearful and destructive enemy, the super-pious, self-right-
eous "good" member. Despite the unquestionable amount of
damage done the Church by the inroads of worldliness, it is
quite possible that an equal amount of damage has been done by
those who have deceived themselves into thinking that their
goodness reaches unto heaven. There is no sin so subtly dangerous as the self-sufficiency of the morally religious man. "Goodness" can be exalted so highly in one's own thinking that it
actually becomes a barrier to reconciliation with God. In Jesus'
parable of the Pharisee and the publican the sin of the Pharisee
was in thinking his tower reached higher than it did.

High-sounding moral principles are often an unconscious effort to clothe self-interest with the stature of a Tower of Babel
and thus to claim for them an eminence they do not possess.
Imperialism is called "the white man's burden." Both labor and
management strive in all sincerity to maintain or advance widely
divergent economic patterns as being "the American way."
Social and physical scientists hail developments that make religion
a minor matter of mere cultural value and God an outdated
anachronism. The feudal lords of the thirteenth century in
Europe finally fell to the bolshevists of that day, the business-
men in the cities that grew up around the castle walls; but all
the while they protested that they were protecting not *their*
civilization but civilization as such. The tenth anniversary number of the bulletin of the League of Fighting Godless in Russia
contained this expression of human pride: "The Stakhanov
movement [a plan for piecework in factories] must play an out-
standing role in the overthrow of religion. It signifies a mighty
increase in the power of man, who is conquering nature and

breaking down all previously imposed standards. If the scholars of the bourgeois world maintain that there are limits beyond which man's perception and man's strength cannot go, that there are matters which a limited intelligence will not perceive, it is evident that under the proletarian deliverance from religion the creation of conscious workers in a classless society can, with the aid of the latest technical acquisitions, proceed to tasks which man, fettered by religion, would never have dared to face. In a socialist society knowledge is free from narrow limits. Man can learn everything and conquer everything. There is no bulwark which bolshevists cannot take by storm." [6]

In an essay in his book *Beyond Tragedy* Reinhold Niebuhr cites a number of historical illustrations of the fact that "one of the most pathetic aspects of human history is that every civilization expresses itself most pretentiously, compounds its partial and universal values most convincingly, and claims immortality for its finite existence at the very moment when the decay which leads to death has already begun." [7] Plato projected the perspectives of the Greek city-state into a universally valid political ideal and turned to Sparta for his model because of Spartan unity and cohesion. But that unity was the fruit of militarism that merely arrested social decay until a more sudden and violent disintegration took place. The Egyptian pyramids, the unconscious claim of a whole civilization to have achieved immortal power, were built in a period when Egyptian civilization "was ripe to the point of overripeness." The building of the pyramids accentuated the injustices of the slavery upon which Egyptian civilization was built, and thus hastened the decay they were intended to defy. The Justinian Code of Roman law, the pride of Roman civilization, "was completed in a period when the Roman Empire was already dead, though not yet buried." In the thirteenth century Thomas Aquinas drew the strands of medieval culture together in one imposing synthesis that seemed the outline of a permanent culture and a universal civilization. "Yet the thirteenth century was not only the greatest but also the last of the medieval centuries." The Empire State Building in New York, perfect symbol of the pride of a commercial civilization, was completed just as the great depression came. A new League of Nations building in Geneva was completed just in time to hear a vain plea for justice from the Emperor of Abyssinia, and that failure of the nations to act in effective collectiveness furnished the trigger for collapse of the League.

Recent years have seen the erection of the impressive United Nations building in New York. Often it has seemed to be another Tower of Babel as divisive human pride and selfishness have been carried into it. It can become a monument to disunity and doom, and it will become such if there is nothing to proclaim in its halls but national advantage and human greed. The noblest dreams of great men are enshrined in the purposes for which it was built, but human wisdom alone cannot bring enduring peace and world unity. Somehow this agency must reflect the purposes of God or it will be but the grandest Tower of Babel yet built.

So, far from making the "name" that would rival and surpass the sovereign dominion of God, the Tower of Babel has become the symbol of man's disunity. The story emphasizes the fact that it is man's exaltation of himself as over against God that is the prime cause of divisions and rivalries, of which the different languages are symbolic. The symbolism is perfect, for nothing is a better representation of both the glory and the frailty of man than language. The gift of language, with its accompanying blessing of communication with one another in the present and of profiting from the past and of preserving wisdom for the future, is man's great treasure and a supreme differentiation from the animals. Each language bears imperishable treasures of the human heart, but it is also freighted with the long, sad history of man's conflicts and misunderstandings. Cross a border between nations speaking different languages, and the difference is so great as to be almost a physical blow. In many cases, were it not for the fact that each language had for centuries carried biased records of past conflicts between the two peoples and nurtured and preserved jealously distinctive customs and traditions, the boundary would long since have ceased to exist. According to a story whose accuracy I am unable to check but which seems to be well authenticated, the war with Japan would have been shortened by many weeks had it not been for the mistranslation of one word of a dispatch sent through intermediaries to authorities in the United States. Such a thing could happen only because of the difficulty men have in understanding one another, a difficulty both symbolized and heightened by diversity of language.

This Tower of Babel story is in some ways the most philosophic of all the stories we have studied. The whole story expresses a sense of guilt, which is the fruit of a profound insight into the glory and the frailty of the human spirit. Men cannot speak to one another in a common tongue because they have no common interest or mutual regard. Sometimes when a person wishes to emphasize a wide gulf between himself and someone else, he says, "He doesn't speak my language." We know at once what is meant by that expression. Language is the enshrinement of the world in which each of us lives. "Out of the abundance of the heart his mouth speaketh," was the remark of Jesus on the subject.[8] The expression of thoughts in language reveals how far apart or how close we dwell to one another.

We have said that this story is quite philosophic, but one may lay aside all subtleties, interpret the narrative very literally, and arrive at the same basic lesson. In intense pride and self-sufficiency the people started to build. But when you adopt the principle of pride, where are you going to stop? Having spurned God's purpose, each man burned with zeal to accomplish his own purpose. When selfishness is given free reign, it never stops until the self is exalted above all others. With the conception of a majestic, sovereign God dispensed with, each man became as a god in his own sight; and, to his way of thinking, the world revolved around him and his plans. So strife grew among the people. No man could understand his neighbor because he did not want to understand him; he was concerned only that the neighbor yield to *his* purpose. So factions grew and bitter dissension developed, and in anger group after group departed, eager to put as much distance as possible between them and their now-alienated brethren.

Such may have been the succession of events. The familiar Hebraism of attributing the dispersion of the people to an immediate act of God is a common Old Testament characteristic. Whether the story is read as literal history or as philosophic symbolism, it is impossible to read anything into it other than a picture of a fatal weakness of man that extends to even his highest aspirations.

The perfect counterpart and reversal of this event is the story of Pentecost in Acts 2. In Jerusalem on that day was a gathering "out of every nation under heaven." Yet, listening to the ecstatic utterances of a group of unlearned Galileans, this polyglot mass of disunited mankind cried out in amazement, "Parthians, and Medes, and Elamites, and the dwellers in Mesopotamia, and in Judaea, and Cappadocia, in Pontus, and Asia, Phrygia, and Pamphylia, in Egypt, and in the parts of Libya about Cyrene, and strangers of Rome, Jews and proselytes, Cretes and Arabians, we do hear them speak in our tongues the wonderful works of God." The lesson is vividly obvious. When men in their pride and self-interest boast of their achievements, Babel results; they are "Parthians, Medes, Elamites . . . " But when they declare "the wonderful works of God," human distinctions, divisions, and languages cease to be barriers and become agents of a common purpose and over-arching Will.

The virtually negligible progress of an artificially created language such as Esperanto is evidence of the fact that languages are but symptoms and symbols of deeper divisions. Some superficial help may come from a new, universal language; but when common interests between people develop, the barriers of language are readily broken down. Greek was the world-language of the time of Christ, for the military domination of Alexander the Great had established community of interests over a wide area, and the language remained long after the military power had vanished. Today English is readily used throughout most of the world, and, significantly, is best understood in those areas most closely tied in interests to the United States and Great Britain. But when zealous patriots wish to fan the flames of nationalism, as, for example, in Eire and the Scottish Highlands, great stress is laid on reviving or preserving their ancient language. The story of Babel is actually a deep confession of guilt, the guilt of human pride setting itself arrogantly to selfish aims instead of to joyous devotion to the will of God. It is a confession that man is mortal, while God is divine.

Babel is the climax of the stories in the early chapters of Genesis. It portrays the finite limitations of even the highest reaches of man's spirit. Climb as high as he may, man may not cross the gulf fixed between the Creator and the creature. With the stage thus set, with every effort of man thwarted in trying to lift himself from his deathbed of sin, there begins in Genesis 12 with Abraham the long, patient story of God's dealing with this problem. From the story of man's disunity the whole Bible from this point moves along the record of God's re-gathering mankind into one family until the shout breaks forth, "The kingdom of the world has become the kingdom of our Lord and of his Christ, and he shall reign for ever and ever." [9]

NOTES AND ACKNOWLEDGMENTS

NOTES AND
ACKNOWLEDGMENTS

Chapter II—In the Beginning God

1. Reprinted from Claude Moore Fuess, *Daniel Webster*, Vol. 2, p. 410. Boston: Little, Brown and Company, 1930.

2. H. H. Farmer, *God and Men*, p. 79. New York: Abingdon-Cokesbury Press, 1947. By permission of Abingdon Press.

3. Paul Tillich, *The New Being*, p. 121. New York: Charles Scribner's Sons, 1955. Used by permission.

4. J. S. Whale, *Christian Doctrine*, p. 32. London and New York: Cambridge University Press, 1941. Used by permission.

5. II Corinthians 5:17. (Author's translation.)

6. *The Westminster Confession of Faith*, Ch. III, Sec. I.

7. Acts 17:28. (R.S.V.) This and other quotations from the Revised Standard Version of the Bible are copyright 1946 and 1952 by the Division of Christian Education of the National Council of the Churches of Christ in the United States of America.

8. Genesis 1:26-27; 2:7. Unless otherwise noted, all Scripture quotations are from the King James Version of the Bible.

9. Genesis 1:26-28.

10. Ralph W. Sockman, *Now to Live*, p. 128. New York: Abingdon-Cokesbury Press, 1946. By permission of Abingdon Press. (Punctuation altered slightly.)

11. Oliver Martin, *Two Educators: Hutchins and Conant*, Human Affairs Pamphlets. Chicago: Henry Regnery Company, 1948. Used by permission.

Chapter III—The Garden of Eden

1. Reginald Heber, in "From Greenland's Icy Mountains," 1879. (For this line see *Psalms and Hymns*, Presbyterian Committee of Publication, Richmond, Va., 1901.)

2. Henry F. Lyte, in "Abide With Me," 1847.

3. Genesis 3:6. (R.S.V.)

4. D. R. Davies, *Down Peacock's Feathers*, p. 49. New York: The Macmillan Company, 1944.

5. *The Westminster Shorter Catechism*, Answer to Question 14.

6. Genesis 2:25.

7. Walter Russell Bowie, Exposition of the Book of Genesis in *The Interpreter's Bible*, Vol. I, p. 507. Nashville: Abingdon Press, 1952. By permission.

8. Scarlett, William (Editor), *Phillips Brooks: Selected Sermons,* p. 117. New York: E. P. Dutton & Co., Inc., 1949.

9. Genesis 3:16. (R.S.V.)

10. See II Corinthians 5:17. (R.S.V.)

11. Genesis 3:24. (R.S.V.)

12. J. S. Whale, *op. cit.,* p. 50. By permission.

13. *Ibid.,* p. 52.

14. II Corinthians 9:15.

Chapter IV—The Tale of the City of Beginning

1. Marcus Dods, "The Book of Genesis" in *The Expositor's Bible,* p. 16. Grand Rapids: Wm. B. Eerdmans Publishing Co., 1947.

2. Genesis 4:22. (Author's translation.)

3. Lincoln Barnett, "The Coming of Civilization," Courtesy LIFE Magazine, June 4, 1956, p. 80. Copyright 1956 Time Inc.

4. Genesis 4:23-24. Verse 23 as translated by George Adam Smith, in *The Early Poetry of Israel,* p. 21. (Schweich Lectures, 1910.) Quoted in D. M. G. Stalker (*Genesis i.-xii,* published by The Church of Scotland Publications Department, 1950), who adds his own translation of verse 24.

Chapter V—The Wages of Sin

1. Jude 6. See also II Peter 2:4.

2. Romans 8:22.

3. Genesis 6:5, 11-12.

4. Isaiah 11:6-9. (K.J.V., with R.S.V. rendering of "adder's den.")

5. I Peter 3:20-21.

6. I Corinthians 3:9.

7. Genesis 8:21.

8. Genesis 6:12.

9. Alan Richardson, *Genesis I-XI,* p. 106. London: S.C.M. Press Ltd., 1953. Used with the permission of The Macmillan Company, distributors in the United States.

10. *Ibid.,* p. 114.

11. Genesis 1:28.

Chapter VI—Pride Goeth Before a Fall

1. Genesis 10:2. See also 10:5 and 10:31.

2. Genesis 6:9. (K.J.V. margin.)

3. Lincoln Barnett, *op. cit.,* p. 100. By permission.

4. Reinhold Niebuhr, *Beyond Tragedy,* p. 28. New York: Charles Scribner's Sons, 1937, 1946. Used by permission.

5. Reinhold Niebuhr, *op. cit.,* pp. 28, 29, 35.

6. Quoted by Niebuhr, *op. cit.,* pp. 37-38.

7. See Niebuhr, *op. cit.,* pp. 39-41.

8. See Luke 6:45.

9. Revelation 11:15. (R.S.V.)